IMPROVE YOUR MEMORY

POWER OF THE THIRD EYE

Comments about the Book

"This is the only book, which comprehensively analyses the human memory system and systematically presents the techniques of memory programming with special focus on student's requirements".

— Rajrup Fuliya, IAS
Vice Chancellor, CDL University, Sirsa

"Science of Memory is well defined and simplified in this book".

— Biswaroop Roy Chowdhury
Guinness World Record holder as strongest memory man

"Mystery of human memory system is revealed. It is an eye opener for all of us".

— Rajesh Thakkar and Sucheta Thakkar
(Living Calculators)
Limca Book Record holders as first Indian couple to memorise mathematical tables up to one lakh

"This book enlightens unknown self to a well-known self".

— B K Ashok Gaba
National co-ordinator of Security Services Wing of Rajyoga Education and Research Foundation

"Besides enhancing memory power, this book is also helpful to rediscover the real-self".

— B K Asha
Associate Editor, Purity
Director, Om Shanti Retreat Centre, and National co-ordinator of Administrative Wing of Rajyoga Education and Research Foundation

Improve *Your* Memory

Power of the third eye

B K Chandra Shekhar
Guinness World Record Holder

MP
MAHAVEER PUBLISHERS

Published by
MAHAVEER PUBLISHERS
4764/2A, 23-Ansari Road, Daryaganj
New Delhi - 110002
Ph. : 011 – 66629669–79–89
Fax : 011 – 41563419
e-mail : mahaveerpublishers@gmail.com

First Edition : 2009
Third Impression : 2011

Improve Your Memory
ISBN : 9788183520775

Distributed by
VAIBHAV BOOK SERVICE
e-mail : vaibhavbookservice@gmail.com

Printed by Jaico Printers, New Delhi

Dedicated with
reverence to "GOD",
The Supreme Father of
all Souls, who has been
the perennial source of
inspiration for me.

ACKNOWLEDGMENT

At the outset, I thank my Almighty father—GOD, the father of humanity Pita Shri Brahma Baba and my divine mother Jagdamba Saraswati, who have taught me to use The Third Eye for digging out the treasures of knowledge and wisdom from the memory bank. I also take this opportunity to express my gratitude to revered BK Dadi Dr. Prakash Mani (Chief of Brahmakumaris), BK Dadi Janki, BK Dadi Hridayamohini, Brother BK Nirwair and Brother BK Ashok Gaba for their kind blessings and encouragement.

I am very grateful to Shri Rajrup Fuliya, IAS (Commissioner, Hisar Division and Vice Chancellor of Choudhary Devilal University, Sirsa), for writing a learned foreword and making useful suggesions. I am also grateful to Mr. Biswaroop Roy Choudhary (the strongest memory mind of India), who taught me memory techniques, to BK Ranjit Fuliya and Prof. Ved Guliani for all help and editing the book, to BK Satbir, artist, Gyan Sarovar, Mt. Abu and Shri Braj Kishore Singh, Graphic Designer, who helped in composing and designing the book.

I specially thank the young, energetic Manager of Mahaveer Publishers, Shri Dilip Kumar Jha, who has brought out the book so soon and so decently.

I am also thankful to sister BK Anita, my parents and family members specially my wife Reeta, my youngest brother Vijayshanker and sister Vidya, my friends, Shri Dhirendra Pratap Singh, Mr. Krishna Arora, Mr. Vikki Arora and Mr. Gaurav Bhatnagar for all help and their best wishes.

B K Chandra Shekhar
E-mail: *shekhar830@yahoo.co.in*

PREFACE

We have infinite riches within our reach. To gain them, all we have to do is to open our third eye or divine eye or divine intellect and behold the treasure house of infinity within us. There is a storehouse within us from which we can extract everything we need to live life gloriously, joyously and peacefully.

A magnetised piece of iron can lift about twelve times its own weight but if demagnetised it won't be able to lift even a feather. In the same way the people who have magnetic power in their third eye live their lives with full faith and confidence but those who have not opened up yet their third eye, grope in the dark and remain full of fears and doubts.

Everything in this world has been created twice. First it is created and visualised by The Third eye and after that it came into reality which we see through our physical eye. Take the examples of inventions. All inventions first took place in the third eye and the power of third eye discovered the know-how from its subconscious mind and carried out several researches first mentally and then practically to invent the things in reality. Thus the power of third eye is wonderful. At present, laymen use this power less than 1%, intellectuals use this power upto 3%, scientists, researchers, analysts use this power upto 10% and only a very few people for instance Albert Einstein used his power of the third eye upto 17 %.

What motivated me to write this book is a deep desire to share the facts, which have been gathered from various sources and the results of my own experiments in the field of human memory system.

I have tried to explain the great fundamental truths of human mind. Although psychologists and mind experts have explained it partially in their own languages, I have tried to explain it in common man's language which can be easily understood by anyone.

The universal truth is that we all are immortal souls. Till we souls remain in the physical body, we refer to this body by telling it is my body. It means I am different from this body and this body belongs to me. Even the subtle organs of self i.e. Mind, Intellect and Impressions of memory, all belong to me. It means I am the powerful soul. It is quite absurd telling that my mind is powerful or my subconscious mind is powerful which belong to me and I am weak. It is in fact 'I' am the powerful soul and these subtle organs belong to me and I am the master of these organs. I keep controlling my mind with the help of my intellect, which is also known as third eye. When this third eye is diseased, it becomes powerless. And when the control-instrument becomes defective, 'I' soul, feels incapacitated to handle my conscious or sub conscious mind. This is the plain truth: unless we make our 'Third Eye' powerful, we are not going to be the master of our mind. Conscious mind and subconscious mind will keep ruling on us till we souls keep telling that we are weak and our mind is powerful.

Just compare Mind with a horse that has its own memory (subconscious mind) and the Intellect is the bridle by which horse is controlled and soul is the rider of the mind-horse. Soul controls the mind-horse with the bridle of intellect. But in the present scenario soul has forgotten that it is infact a rider. It is weakened since the bridle has been dropped by the soul. Soul is unaware of the bridle and is being dragged by the horse, which is galloping with its own memory. And soul feels incapacitated, frustrated and depressed because it has lost its real and powerful identity.

Through this book I have tried to explain this simple fact to all human beings and also explained the practical steps to be taken to catch hold of the bridle (The control system faculty – Intellect) and tighten it so that your mind horse comes on the right track and moves according to rider's wish and not with its own memory. In other words I can say that Intellect is the eye of the soul (Third eye or Divine eye) through which soul discriminates and decides the matter or things appearing on the screen of mind.

"ONLY A POWERFUL THIRD EYE CAN MAKE A SOUL POWERFUL".

Therefore I have titled the book "Power of The Third Eye".

The power of third eye can play a major role in our life in the following ways

- It develops concentration power.
- It improves our long term memory power.
- It develops a positive personality.
- It plays great role in Stress Management enabling one to lead a tension free life.
- It develops self-confidence.
- It helps us to learn with fun.
- It helps to develop creativity and inventions.
- It makes our life interesting and optimistic.
- It provides energy to remove boredom and laziness in life.
- It creates a superior vision.
- It makes life purposeful.
- It helps students to prepare for examination thoroughly and removes examination phobia.
- It helps to compete with others and succeed.
- It helps to cure sickness and several psychosomatic diseases.
- It develops a holistic approach for physical, mental, social and spiritual growth.
- It removes inferiority complex and develops powers to face, discriminate and judge.
- It make us powerful from within.

Before I close, I wish to share with my readers that I have experienced the power of the third eye in my personal life. Like most of us I faced many depressing situations. Physically I suffered from cancer, hepatitis-C, fibrosis of lever and diabetes. I met with serious accidents also. Many a time I stood in utter darkness. I coped with the darkness wth the power of the third eye and got unbelievably great results. The diseases were gone and I bacame a normal person. My memory is fantastic now. In this book I share the crux of my experiments and conclusions of my experiences.

Read this book carefully, earnestly and lovingly. It will definitely help you to open and empower your third eye.

FOREWORD

RAJ RUP FULIYA, IAS
Divisional Commissioner, Hisar

Office of the Vice Chancellor, CDL University, Sirsa

Raj Rup Fuliya, IAS
Commissioner, Hisar Division and
Vice Chancellor, CDL University, Sirsa

| Presently Commissioner & secretary to Govt. Haryana |

When we speak of weaknesses or strengths of a person, we often refer to his intellect. When we pray to God, we ask for powers from Him, which also refer to a powerful intellect. The expression "Will Power" is often used to refer our ability to put our ideals into practice. We know what is beneficial and what is harmful, but choosing the right activity is directly related to soul's intellectual strength.

Intellect is a faculty of soul through which it selects the desired thoughts and emotions. The intellect performs three important functions i.e. to visualize, to discriminate and to decide. Out of these, the power to visualize is the most important function of the intellect. That is why intellect is also known as "Divine Eye or Third Eye".

A soul with a powerful intellect can enjoy the experience of its own choice regardless of external stimuli, whereas a soul with a weak intellect is often pushed by the strong impressions or habits stored in subconscious mind. It can also be influenced by the moods of the other or by atmosphere around. That is why many psychologists say that our subconscious mind/unconscious mind is very powerful and it gets the things done automatically. The title of the book "Power of Third Eye" is justified because it is the intellect which rules the mind and it is the principal faculty of the soul. The power of visualisation programmes the subconscious mind and hence the powers of third eye certainly play a vital role in shaping one's attitude and altitude of personality.

This book consists of two sections. Section - I is related to self realisation and understanding the real concept of human memory system and Section II provides very interesting techniques on enhancing the memory power. This book differs from other books (presently available in the market on memory) in following respects:

1. This is the only book, which comprehensively analyses the human memory system with respect to the power of soul where as other books relate the functions of memory entirely with the process of the brain mechanism. Brain is just an instrument for recording but the mind and intellect (the two faculties of soul) play the vital role in memory programming.

2. This book systematically presents the techniques of memory programming with special focus on students' requirement. Section – II of this book is very interesting for students and can be easily grasped by them. They can take maximum benefits of these techniques as enumerated in this book.

3. This book also specially focuses on the importance of Rajyoga meditation, which enhances tremendously one's concentration and memory power. This is also my personal experience. I have been practising Rajyoga meditation since my teenage which has helped me a lot to increase concentration power and pursue my goals during my student life. No other book has explained its importance so far.

B K Chandra Shekhar is known to me personally for the last ten years. He is a simple man with high thinking. He had lots of experiences of applying the power of third eye. He applied these powers to get rid of life threatening diseases like cancer, hepatitis and diabetes. His services are sought from various schools, colleges, social organisations, institutions and Central/State govt. He conducts memory work shop for students and professionals. He also provides tips to students to remove their exam fear and better their performances. He is the visiting faculty to the "Academy for a Better World", Mount Abu, Rajsthan.

He has put sincere efforts to present this precious knowledge of memory system in a book form worth emulating for the benifits of student community. His efforts are an eye opener for all of us. I hope this book will certainly prove beneficial for the students in opening their third eye and in enhancing their memory power and help them to harness their talents and release their true potential. I wish him in this hard endeavour and many successes in his life.

(RAJ RUP FULIYA)

CONTENTS

SECTION II

MEMORY TECHNIQUES

HUMAN - BEING
TWO DIFFERENT REALITIES

Ten students were crossing the river. After they crossed, they wanted to carry out a check to ensure that everyone had safely crossed the river. All of them came and stood in a single line. One of them came out and started counting. He could find only 9 people. All of them got upset, because there was one less person.

Another person came out of the line and started counting. He too could find only 9 people. They could not find the 10th person. They confirmed that the 10th person might have got drowned.

At that time, a saint was passing by the side of the river. He heard their problem and counted the people in the line. He then turned his finger towards the person who was counting and arrived at a total of 10. He said that the 10th person was none other than the person who was counting the rest of them.

Similarly we never count ourselves and think that we are the body only. We never differentiate ourselves from the body and even introduce ourselves with name, age, colour, sex, caste, occupation etc. of our physical body. One has to find and know the self to know the real mystery of life.

(I) HUMAN BEING- NOT ONE BUT TWO

When I say – I am Ram or Rahman, I mean the name of my body by which I am identified and called. If I say my father, my brother, wife or friend, it indicates their relationship with me. When I say my house, my car, my table, all these indicate my belongings; when I say I am a doctor, an engineer or a teacher, it indicates the acquired scientific and systematic knowledge for becoming a professional to earn livelihood. When I say my head, my ears, my eyes, I mean these are the organs of my body. My relations, my body, my possessions are different from me though they belong to me. I make different uses of my body and its organs. Even the brain cannot think, decide, perceive and perform on it own. It is an inanimate component of the 'being', which performs these functions with the help of the brain and gross body. As all goods are meant for others' use, similarly the physical body is not created for its own use. It is for the use of the conscient entity known as 'being or soul.' The soul is a sparkling point of conscient energy that empowers the entire body to monitor and perform all physical activities. The soul harmonizes the growth of body. When the soul(the master) leaves the body, the latter loses its awareness, ability to think, decide, act, react and experience including all bodily functions and ceases with the departure of 'being' from human.

So soul is the life force in the living human body. It is situated in the centre of the forehead in level with hypothalamus and close to the sense organs and acts through them. In layman's language, soul lives in the middle of the forehead. That is why most people in India apply 'tilak' or 'bindi' on their forehead, as it is true symbol of the self being in the forehead.

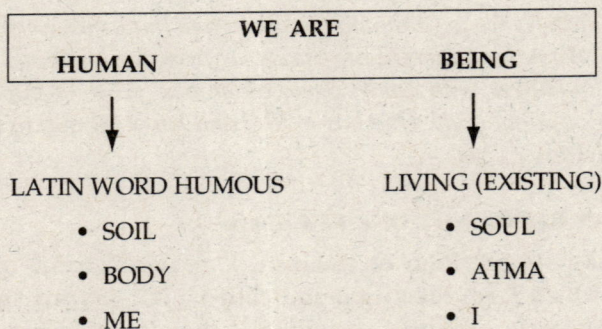

WE ARE	
HUMAN	BEING
↓	↓
LATIN WORD HUMOUS	LIVING (EXISTING)
• SOIL	• SOUL
• BODY	• ATMA
• ME	• I

Albert Einstein said, "Science without spirituality is blind and spirituality without science is lame." Both Lame and Blind want to have a taste of grapes but can not until both co-operate and co-ordinate with each other.

The basic study of science revolves round Atoms. The word 'Atom' has come from a Greek word called Atomos, which means indivisible or a thing which can not be further sub divided. Atom is the smallest non-living physical entity. From the very same word Atomos the word ATMA has also come which means the smallest living metaphysical entity. Life of a human being is the perfect example of the blend of Atoms and Atma

The word 'Human' has come from a Latin word 'Humous' which means Soil which is further made up of

ATOMOS (A GREEK WORD WHICH MEANS UNDIVISIBLE)

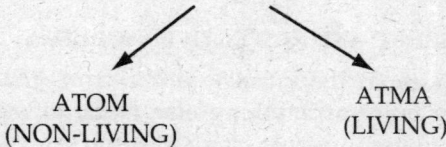

ATOM
(NON-LIVING)

ATMA
(LIVING)

millions of atoms and our body or me is made up of more than 60 trillions of these atoms. The word 'Being' as per dictionary means any thing which is existing, which is I or ATMA or Soul.

(II) SYSTEM OF HUMAN BEING

There are two systems of human being. These are:

a. System of Human
b. System of Being (Inner System)

(a) SYSTEM OF HUMAN AND THEIR RESPECTIVE FUNCTIONING ORGANS

There are eight systems in human body. Each system of human body has got its respective organs to function. For example, bones and muscles for skeleton system, billion of neurons and brain for nervous system, lungs for respiratory system, heart for circulatory system, stomach for digestive system, all glands for secretion of hormones and enzymes for endocrine system, sex organs for reproductive system and so on. It is well understood by the following table.

SYSTEM OF HUMAN BODY	RESPECTIVE ORGANS
1. Skeleton system	Bones and muscles
2. Nervous system	Brain & neurons
3. Respiratory system	Lungs
4. Circulatory system	Heart
5. Digestive system	Stomach
6. Endocrine system	All glands
7. Reproductive & immune system	Reproductive organs & WBC
8. Excretory system	Skin & excretory organs

(b) SYSTEM OF "BEING" AND RESPECTIVE FACULTIES

The unique thing about the intrinsic abilities *of BEING* is that no other physical body or anything else made of matter (like computer or calculator) possess these abilities except the soul. These are:

(1) The ability to think or wish or will or to create emotions through conscious mind. (In Hindi called –Mann). This is **thought system** of human being.

(2) The ability to analyse, understand or investigate, visualize or realize and to judge through intellect (in Hindi called-Buddhi). This is **control system** of being.

(3) The ability to retain impressions of past thoughts in the form of attitudes, moods, habits or resolves (in Hindi called *sanskars*) in its memory bank (known as subconscious mind and unconscious mind). This is **memory system** of being.

This is explained by the following table.

SYSTEM OF BEING	RESPECTIVE FACULTIES
Thought system	Conscious Mind
Control system	Intellect
Memory system	Sub-conscious Mind & Unconscious Mind

1. THOUGHT SYSTEM BY CONSCIOUS MIND

Conscious mind is one of the faculties of the soul, which receives and creates thoughts and emotions. It receives thoughts and emotions either from sense organs of the body (eyes, ears, nose, tongue and skin) or from internal faculties called subconscious or unconscious mind.

2. CONTROL SYSTEM BY INTELLECT

The faculty by which the soul can select its desired thoughts and emotions is INTELLECT

The expressions "will power" is often used to refer our ability to put our ideas into practice. We know it be for our well-being and to resist activity, which is harmful. This is directly related to soul's intellectual strength. When we speak of weakness or strength of the soul, we are referring to the intellect. In the case of weak soul it is almost as if the intellect plays no part in determining which thoughts should arise in the mind, but they seem to come as if pushed by the impressions of subconscious mind or are triggered by the atmosphere around or the moods of others. On the contrary, a powerful soul enjoys the experience of its own choice regardless or external stimuli.

Thus, intellect performs three functions:

- Analyse, discern and discriminate
- Visualise several images related to the thoughts
- Judge or decide.

In other words, we can say that the intellect is gifted by soul with three powers:

POWER TO DISCRIMINATE, POWER TO VISUALISE AND POWER TO JUDGE

Out of these three powers, power to visualise is the most important. That is why intellect is also called 'the third eye' or 'eye' of knowledge and this is the eye of soul.

3. MEMORY SYSTEM BY MEMORY BANK

Now let us see the last faculty the subconscious mind and unconscious mind, which is called memory bank. Impressions of every action, observation and visualisation in Subconscious Mind are called Memory.

In Sanskrit language, these dispositions or unconscious memories, which are the result of previous actions, are called sanskars. It is these, which give unity of the self. The self coordinates the information received from various senses into various parts of the brain and gives to it an experimental unity without which the encoded memory would be meaningless.

Thus, when the conscious personality has its memories at subliminal or infra liminal level then it can be designated as "subconscious" or unconscious mind.

Subconscious mind has the power to do anything on the basis of information lying in it. It is the power of the subconscious mind that makes our heart beat about 72 times per minute regularly for up to 100 years. It is well known to psychologists that we can consciously be aware of only 7+-2 items at a time. But our subconscious mind can be aware of a large number of items at a time. For example; at any time, the subconscious mind is aware of many body functions including blood pressure, heartbeats, body temperature, chemical balances, blood flow, taking care of emergencies etc. **The subconscious mind is not under our conscious control.**

Requirement of Human Body and Being

Requirement of 'Body' is quantitative: *Food, Cloth and Shelter.*

Requirement of 'Being' (Soul) is qualitative as follows:

(a) PRIMARY QUALITIES

We are originally a point of sentient light fully charged with spiritual (metaphysical) energy that naturally manifests as truth (knowledge), peace, love, Joy, purity, power and bliss (balance) when we first come into this world. *These innate qualities or attributes of the soul are so basic that they themselves are the basis of all virtues and powers.*

TRUTH

An original attribute of the soul and the Supreme soul is the true knowledge of the self, the supreme and the 'eternal drama'. It is represented by the primary *colour – indigo.*

PEACE

An original attribute of the soul and the Supreme soul is peace, which is represented by the primary *colour – Blue*

LOVE

Another original attribute of the soul and the Supreme soul is love, which is represented by *Green Colour – a mixture of blue and yellow.*

JOY OR HAPPINESS

Yet another original attribute of the Soul and the Supreme soul is joy or happiness, which is represented by *Yellow, a primary colour.*

PURITY

It is the original attribute of the Soul and the Supreme soul. It is represented by *Orange colour – a mixture of yellow and red.* Hence, in the state of purity there is a balance of power and joy.

SPIRITUAL POWER

Another original attribute of the Soul and the Supreme soul is power, which is represented by the *primary colour – Red. The eight powers are different shades of red colour.*

BLISS

The core attribute of the Soul and the Supreme Soul is represented by *Violet colour – a mixture of Red and Indigo.* Hence, *in this state of being we are in a state of balance between truth and power. A blissful soul is full of both wisdom and spiritual powers.*

(b) THE SECONDARY QUALITIES OF THE SOUL

Virtues are secondary qualities springing from myriad combinations of the seven basic attributes mentioned above. Another aspect of the *secondary qualities, which come into play more frequently in our day-to-day life, is that these are linked to human relationship.*

These are as follows:

Discipline	Introvertness	Tirelessness	Detachment
Honesty	Self-confidence	Appreciation	Obedience
Generosity	Humility	Determination	Farsightedness
Orderliness	Sweetness	Fearlessness	Aloofness
Reality	Serenity	Egolessness	Purity
Good wish	Coolness	Sobriety	Mercifulness
Truthfulness	Contentment	Worrylessness	Asceticism
Politeness	Simplicity	Benevolence	Observer state
Equality	Tolerance	Co-operation	Royalty

SCIENCE OF BEING

As the *study of the system of human body* is called *physical science*, in the same manner the *study of being* is called *meta-physical science*, which is also known as spiritual science.

Just like an **ATOM** is made up of protons, electrons and neutrons, similarly ATMA consists of three faculties called conscious mind, Intellect, and subconscious mind.

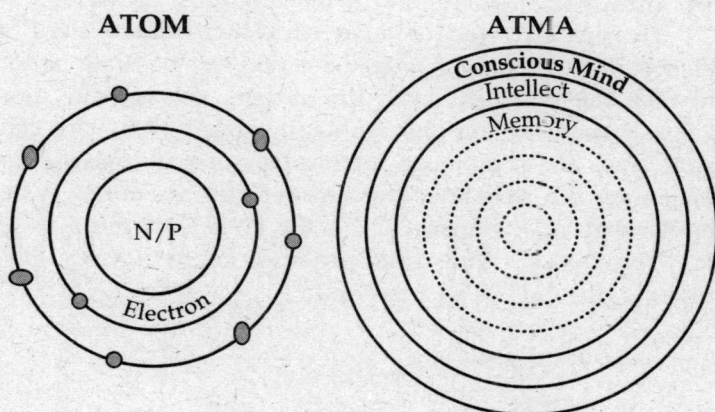

ATOM   **ATMA**

Study of Atoms is Science & Study of Atma is called
Spiritual Science.

INTEGRATED ACTIONS BY ALL THREE SYSTEMS OF BEING

Five sense organs by which conscious mind receives information in the form of Thoughts, Emotions and Desires are received by intellect where they are analysed, visualised, and judged for the best possible actions. And then the body executes the actions through the motor organs. Now these actions are again observed by the sense organs and are registered as impressions in the memory systems or the subconscious mind. This memory system supplies data and information to the conscious mind as and when registered. And this process keeps taking place automatically day-in and day-out.

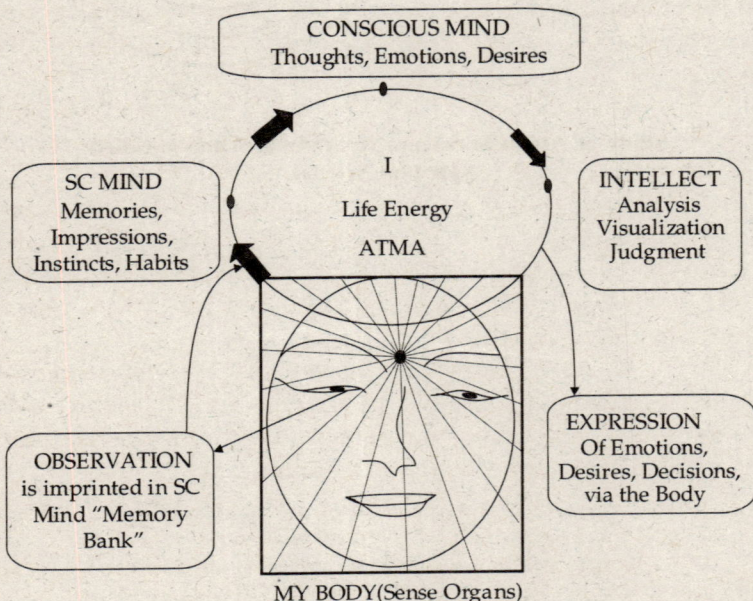

CONSCIOUS MIND
Thoughts, Emotions, Desires

SC MIND
Memories,
Impressions,
Instincts, Habits

I
Life Energy
ATMA

INTELLECT
Analysis
Visualization
Judgment

OBSERVATION
is imprinted in SC
Mind "Memory
Bank"

EXPRESSION
Of Emotions,
Desires, Decisions,
via the Body

MY BODY(Sense Organs)

Let us take the example of a person learning to drive a car for the first time. The conscious mind through the sense organs gathers information about the techniques of driving. These are analysed, visualised and judged by the control system and the driving action is taken by the motor organs like hand, legs etc. These actions are observed by the sense organs and impression of driving technique is registered in our memory or subconscious mind. From now onwards, the information to the conscious mind is fed both by subconscious mind and sense organs and to our surprise, after some time Subconscious Mind feeds 95% of the information and remaining 5% is fed by the sense organs.

Imagine a situation during learning how to drive a car, when the instructor switches on the music system on the first day itself. The pupil finds it hard to concentrate and he will find the music to be a disturbance. But after few days when he becomes comfortable, without music he will get bored and ask for it. The reason is very simple when the subconscious mind takes over, sense organs remains idle. This is the reason why a person goes to the bathroom automatically after waking up in the morning, or the hand automatically goes to the alarm clock before he goes to sleep.

Out of all these, most important function of intellect is the power of creative visualisation. It is the place where all the inventions have taken place.

Let me give some example to drive home this point. Sir Isaac Newton saw an apple falling from a tree and visualised constantly and creatively why it falls down on the earth instead of going up in the sky? And this led to invent the theory of Gravitation.

It is well known that physicians use the power of visualisation to cure diseases by giving them "Placebo" with no real medicinal values, the patients are told otherwise. And the patients are cured with visualisation only.

A Layman uses less than 1% of power of intellect.
An intellectual uses only 3% of intellect.
Scientists and researchers use only 10% of intellect.
90% of the intellect is still unused.

'IMPRESSIONS' are the genetic coding of the soul: Just as the metabolic activities in the cell body are based on the genetic information held in the nucleus, the quality of mental activities of thoughts, desires, feelings, visions etc. are primarily based on impressions.

'INTELLECT' can change the genetic code of impressions: Just as the cell membrane selectively permit different molecules of nutrients into the cell body, the intellect acts as a screening and monitoring device determining which influences from the environment should be processed and which one to be ignored, it also determines which thoughts, desires, or vision prompted by impressions (sanskars) should be acted upon.

The intellect can change the genetic code of impressions by focusing its attention on the original attributes and causing pure, virtuous thoughts to emerge on the mental screen. It can weaken negative (IMPRESSIONS) sanskaras by not allowing the related thoughts to reach at the level of action. When the power of discrimination of the intellect is weak, the negative sanskaras, the negative vibrations of the environment and moods of other people find easy access on the mind making it very turbulent and peaceless.

OBJECTIVE MIND

Conscious mind and intellect both are known as objective mind because it deals with outward objects. The objective mind is aware of the objective world. Its media of observation is our physical sense. Our intellect, one of the faculties of objective mind is our guide and director in our contact with our environment. We gain knowledge through our five senses. Our objective mind learns through observation, education and its association with past experiences of memory. *The greatest function of the objective mind is performed by intellect that is of reasoning, visualising and decision making.*

SUBJECTIVE MIND

Subconscious mind is also referred as subjective mind. It is aware of its environment, but not by means of physical senses.

It perceives by intuition. It is the seat of emotions and the storehouse of memory. It performs the highest functions when our objective senses are not functioning. In other words it is that intelligence that makes itself known when the objective mind is suspended or in a sleepy or drowsy state or in Alpha, or delta state.

COORDINATION BETWEEN OBJECTIVE AND SUBJECTIVE MIND

When intellect, one of the faculties of objective mind withdraws from conscious mind that is from sensory organ observations and starts using its most important power of visualisation in coordination with subjective mind, there is a drastic reduction in brain waves from beta activities to Alpha, theta, and delta. In Alpha, theta, and delta waves, the third eye elevates itself with the capacity of clairvoyance and clairaudience. It can see and hear events that are taking place elsewhere. Sometimes it leaves our body, travels to a distant lands and brings back information that is often of the most exact and truthful in nature. The third eye with low brain waves can read the thoughts of others, read the contents of sealed envelopes or intuit the information on a computer disc without using disk drive. *These all happens when intellect is deeply connected with subjective mind; that is sub conscious mind, because the subconscious mind has all impressions of past, present and future of our life.* **Intellect with its full potential can even see in the subjective mind, what is going to happen.**

Once we understand the interaction of the objective and subjective minds, we are in a better position to learn the true art of happy and peaceful living.

The habitual thinking of our objective mind establishes deep grooves in our subjective mind. If your habitual thoughts are harmonious, peaceful and constructive, your subjective mind will respond by creating harmony, peace and constructive conditions.

Our objective mind (intellect) or the third eye serves as the watchman at the gate who protects our subjective mind from false impressions. The reason is that our subjective mind is very sensitive to suggestion. It simply reacts to the impressions given to it by our third eye.

TYPES OF BEING-BODY (Inner Body)

Awareness of the self and Body is the basic knowledge. Now let us understand the types of Body of a Soul:

(I) ORIGINAL BODY OR BODY-LESS BODY – [POINT FORM (SEED FORM)]

As the plant grows from a seed, our energy body develops out of point form only. Growth is a physical phenomenon but development a metaphysical phenomena. Development of energy body means developing the image of a perfect personality. *Personality word has come form Greek word "Personas" which means – Mask. As is the mask so is the appearance and characteristic actions taken according to the mask.* Similarly if a person shapes his energy body with an imaginary mask of (divine thoughts & its visualization) divinity and manifests divinity through his character and conduct, he is said to be having a divine personality and if a person manifests devilish character and conduct, he is said to be having personality like a devil. Devil & divine bodies are just like an energy mask covered by a physical body. We have to choose one of them to be a part of our personality.

Swami Vivekananda has said "Education is the manifestation of perfection already in man" and "Religion is the manifestation of divinity already in man."

Religion is known as nature also. As the nature of fire is to burn, nature of ice is to give cooling sensation; similarly the nature of self is peace and purity. Original body (point form) resides in the hypothalamus (seat of soul, where all sensory organs send information and all motor organs get the order to execute the command of soul) of Pituitary gland, which coincides with forehead (between two eyebrows). **It is linked with Agya Chakra which is one of the energy centres in our body.**

(II) ENERGY BODY

This is the inner body covered by a physical body made of bones & flesh. Thought is an energy, which shapes our inner body or energy body. Presence of purity, peace, love, happiness, bliss, power, truth & knowledge (in form of our thoughts, emotions and imagination) make our energy body completely active and dynamic. But lack of any one of the primary virtues deforms and disables our energy body. And deforming of energy body affects the physical body with deformities, disabilities and diseases. This energy body is of five types:

(a) Emotional or Ethereal Body: This type of energy body remains present in children up to the age of 7 years. A child's physical body is more guided by emotions of the childish mind. Healthy environment at home and school shapes the ethereal body of a child. This is the time of physical growth.

(b) Astral Body (Subtle Body): This type of body is shaped after 7 years of age. This body is formed by intellects creativity and visualization power. More creative visualization shapes the child to be a matured adult. This inner body is the basis of all further development of the energy body and a positive personality. Therefore one must take much care of the children after the age of 7 till teenage. After teenage, astral body starts developing into a mental body.

(c) Mental Body: This inner body or energy body is shaped by our thoughts, desires and imaginations. As are our thoughts desires and imagination so would be the mental body, which affects our physical body. All creative act, artistic skills, inventions and innovations take place through mental body. Mental body is called healthy if our thoughts, desires and imaginations are more and more positive and linked to standard file of our memory. Healthy mental body keeps our physical body a healthy one. And negative inner body or deformed mental body due to lack of presence of any one of the primary virtues causes deformities and diseases in the physical body.

(d) Spiritual Body: It is a more healthy and powerful inner body which not only keeps us spiritually and mentally healthy but also keeps us socially and physically healthy. The development of a spiritual body starts from a healthy and positive mental body. Spiritual body indicates the presence of thoughts and imaginations related to primary virtues and all spiritual powers. By this body, not only one can heal his physical body but can also heal others. Positive and powerful radiation through this body creates the vibrations of peace and serenity in surroundings. Many people feel happy and peaceful due to the presence of a spiritual body. It is the state of higher consciousness and shaping of this body is done by meditation exercises.

(e) Cosmic Body: This body is developed from powerful spiritual body. Cosmic body is full of cosmic energy. It can travel beyond body to any place at any point of time by creation of images by one's thoughts and desires. It is ever charged by the Supreme energy (God). Clairvoyance, telekinesis and out of body experience occur through this body only. Cosmic body radiates powerful vibration of all virtues round the clock. Sleeping is not the phenomenon of this body. Cosmic body radiates delta waves all the time and it is the state of balanced emotions and "Yognidra". Cosmic body though covered by the physical body, remains free from the bondages of body, caste, creed, region & religion. It is the state of Supra Consciousness.

Attainment of cosmic body is the real aim and object of all life force (spirit or soul) from where we again become a bodiless body i.e. point of energy. (Like a perfect seed from where a plant of a perfect personality germinates). Shaping of a cosmic body is more done by highest state of meditation exercise, which is a feeling of constant bliss from Supreme power.

INNER BODY AND PHYSICAL BODY RELATIONSHIP

Our inner body is linked up with physical body at seven energy centers with primary virtues, which activate and exercise functional control of the seven systems of our human body. Chakra literally translated means "Wheel of spinning energy". Within our bodies are seven major energy centers. They are located in the front of the spinal column and are aligned vertically up and down the spine. But chakras are aspects of consciousness. *They are not physical, they interact with the physical body through two major vehicles: the endocrine system and the nervous system.* Interestingly enough, the spacing of charkas actually matches major nerve or endocrine centers in the body. All our senses or perceptions can be divided into seven categories, and each of these categories can be associated with a particular chakra. Thus the charkas represent *not only particular parts of our body, but also particular parts of our consciousness.*

Function of Chakras: The function of the chakras is to integrate the physical, emotional, psychological and spiritual faces of a person into a coherent whole. Each of the seven chakras plays a vital functional role in our physical body as well as in our consciousness. The three lower chakras correlate to basic primary needs- *those of survival, procreation and will. The four higher chakras relate to our psychological makeup. They define love, communication and knowledge and can also provide a spiritual connection to this universe and beyond.*

Awakening of Chakras: With attention and understanding we can control and influence our chakras. They can be developed like muscles, programmed like a computer, nurtured like a seed or closed like a book. When a chakra is closed, the life force energy cannot travel through that part of the body. When chakras are awakened and become fully functional, we will be ever evolving towards realisation and integration.

Chakra Psychology: Just, as a massage can soothe an aching muscle or the right nutrient can stimulate a gland to function well, so also the weak or imbalanced chakras can be influenced to function at peak activity. *By reflecting upon the nature of our thoughts, inclinations, perceptions, desires and actions, we can fairly accurately identify which chakras are dormant within us. Chakra psychology is a valuable tool for greater self-understanding.*

Colour, Music and Chakras: Each wheel of energy or chakra has a colour from the rainbow, spins in a clockwise direction and vibrates to a musical note. This representation of the seven vibrations of the different colored chakras happens in a logical and orderly sequence, just like the notes of a musical scale. The heaviest vibration or the longest wavelength is found at the bottom and the lightest on the top. Music played in a certain manner vibrates a particular chakra, and brings out a feeling associated with those musical vibrations. In the similar manner, different colours also represent different parts of our consciousness.

Activating Chakras through Rajyoga: Regular practice of Rajyoga (physically & mentally) stimulates various nerve plexus and glands that lie along the spinal pathway, as well as the spine itself and the ganglionic nerve chains. Over time, an energetic charge builds up in the body and mind. Energy flows more smoothly through the central channel owing to a gradual elimination of obstructions. As this process occurs, physical health and vitality improve, the mind becomes more powerful and one can enter into higher states of meditation with increasing ease.

Seven chakras in our body play a vital role in our total well being. Our chakras get disturbed due to stress and negative emotions, creating disease and disharmony, which prevent us from functioning at our most vibrant and joyful level. The emotions connected with each chakra are guided through meditation techniques to activate and energise each of the chakras.

1. Muladhara (Root) Chakra: The root chakra not only sends energy to bones and muscles of the body but also act as sex center. It is the source of creative energy and power. We are both male and female in our energies, but society does not let us express both.

Most of the societies repress the feminine energy: the left side of the body and the right side of the brain, which is the abode of beauty, stillness, poetry and art. Until age seven, your energy is total. Notice how children are beautiful in their beings. But beyond seven, children are forced to suppress their other side and thus wound their consciousness. In their search for their other half, girls adore their father and boys their mother. Between ages of 7 and 14, the wound can be healed if parents remain most of the time with their children, but if the parents are not there, children look in vain in the outside world for that feminine and masculine energy.

Children in the 14-21 age groups are ready to engage with the opposite sex- to marry- but they are rarely allowed. So they collect and cherish imagination and dreams of the opposite sex through the media. Manufacturers exploit this by selling dreams and sex appeal through their products. And these stuffs play vital role in deforming & disabling the astral and the mental body of youths, which further causes several diseases in the physical body at youthful age of the life. This all leads to further degeneration of their character and conduct. The root chakra is a continuous fountain of positive energy, while our imaginations and expectations are like a huge stone blockings in this marvellous energy fountain. When we burn away all our unwanted imaginations and memories and open ourselves to reality, the creative energy of this chakra flows

2. Swadhisthana (Spleen) Chakra: This chakra is located two inches below the navel and is the place where fear attacks us. The average person has six to 12 fear strokes every 24 hours, while both awake and sleeping. This weakens our immune system and leads to depression, illness, aging, infertility, and impotency. It creates the diseases of kidney also. Fear primarily falls into four categories:

i. Fear of loss of status, wealth or comfort
ii. Fear of disease or loss of a bodily part
iii. Fear of loss of family or friends
iv. Fear of death

Fearlessness is not the absence of fear but it is the courage to face the fear and experience it completely. If we can truly enter into the space of fear and experience it, it can never affect us again so deeply.

3. Manipura (Navel) Chakra: Worry and suppressed emotions sit in the navel center and block this chakra. *"Worrying is nothing but a constant repetition of certain words in the mind"*. This drains away our energy and takes us out of the total awareness and bliss of this moment. Worry is a terrible waste of time, thought and energy. 99% of our worries never come true and the one percent that do, end up being good for us. Many stomach problems; skin diseases and pains are related to the navel center. *Obesity is another byproduct of worry and depression.*

4. Anahata (Heart) Chakra: Unconditional expression of love and affection expands this chakra. Constant need for other's attention and approval blocks it. "Life is a long signature campaign." We are constantly working for social success, rather than individual success. A person working for individual success, even if he fails, will have the satisfaction that he has lived his life. Make a list of all those people who have the power to upset us and realise that we are psychological slaves to these people. The conscious realisation itself will bring about a freedom.

We never know the people who are close to us. We simply form an image of them and continue to relate to that image through out, while the person is in an ever-changing multi-faceted centre of consciousness.

5.Visuddhi (Throat) Chakra: *"Three layers of energy merge in the throat chakra — ordinary physical energy, reserve energy to be used in emergencies and spiritual energy."* We usually use only the first level and forget that there are two more levels behind it; in order to access these levels we need to get rid of our ego, which results in either a superiority or inferiority complex. Comparison and jealousy lock this chakra. When we run in the rat race, the visuddhi closes. Understanding and appreciating our uniqueness opens it. We usually create an idea about our self and compare it to others, which is senseless. If we live our life, we will grow uniquely and will have profound satisfaction, whether or not we have money, fame etc. When we feel tired in our body, we can say "no" and go to the next layer of energy, which will provide us with all the energy, and vitality that we need.

6. Ajna (Brow) Chakra: "Ajna"(AGYA) means will power. We usually spend 80 % of our energy desiring and 20% of our energy to create. These percentages get reversed when this chakra is opened; resulting in fewer desires but more power to create them into reality. Conditioning, labeling and judgements contaminate this chakra. All judgements are prejudiced; they draw conclusions from a few observations (observations are contaminated by our conditioning.) "I am this, you are that, life is this, etc." are statements of the ego. This mental chatter reduces all our experience merely to words.

To live spontaneously and intensely we need to deal with every person and situation without a script. If we trust our being we will have an enormous leap of growth through such spontaneous interaction with the world. Facing life without a script, we will realize that we know much more than we imagine. Whether we believe it or not, like it or not, the fact is that we are God's children and we are same as our father is.

7. Sahasrara (Crown) Chakra: "Sahasrara" means the thousands petal lotus. When this chakra opens, we are flooded with ecstasy and eternal bliss. Discontentment and negativity towards life block this chakra. Gratitude for life and all that God has given us open this chakra. So many blessings are showered upon us and we take them for granted. Our life and our body are amazing gifts from God- absolutely incredible. Living out of deep joy and bliss is the product of simply showing gratitude and respect for the divine. Loving the whole world is easy; loving our neighbour is difficult because it requires actions through acts of gratitude, compassion and affection. Feel gratitude for every small thing in life. *"Gratitude is the greatest attitude which determines our altitude of success in life."*

TABLES OF PRIMARY VIRTUES AND CHAKRA RELATIONSHIP

Primary virtues of pure energy body (Inner body) & related consciousness and colours	Associated human system and related physical or meta-physical elements with virtues	Name of Chakra (Energy Centres in the physical body) associated with Primary Virtues	Position in the body and shape	Diseases in physical body due to lack of associated virtues and deformed mental body
1. Power (Red Colour) relates to our sense of survival & sense of grounding	Skeleton System, Physical Element- Earth	Muladhar Chakra, (Root chakra), or Pelvic or sacral plexus	Between Anus & Genitals, Shape-like Four Petals of Lotus	Diseases like Arthritis, osteoporosis, joints pain, muscular pain, sciatica etc.
2.Purity (Orange Colour) related with consciousness of pro-creation	Reproductive & Immune system, Physical Elements- Water	Swadhisthan Chakra (Hypo gastric or prostrate plexus or spleen chakra)	Between Navel centre & pelvic plexus (Root Chakra), Shape-like Six petals of lotus	Deficiency of immune system, (Aids), Gynecological diseases, problems related to prostate& kidney, and stiff or sore lower back etc.

3. Happiness or Contentment (Yellow colour) associated with control & leadership	Digestive system, Physical Element- Fire	Manipur Chakra (Navel Chakra) or Epigastria or solar plexus	Navel Centre Shape- like **Ten petals of lotus**	Acidity, gastric, peptic ulcers, constipation, gastrointestinal problem, diabetes etc.
4. Love (Green Colour) reflects consciousness of self-less love for all	Blood Circulatory system, Physical Element- Air	Anahat Chakra, (Heart Chakra) Or Cardiac Plexus	Heart, Shape- like **Twelve petals of lotus**	Coronary Arteries diseases, heart attack, angina pain, high B.P, lungs problem, asthma etc.
5. Peace (Sky Blue Colour) associatd with Communication skill and power of speech	Respiratory System, Physical Element- Ether	Vishudha Chakra (Throat Chakra) or Carotid or larynx	Throat, Shape- like **Sixteen petals of lotus**	ENT Problem, stiff neck, cough, colds, thyroid problem etc.
6. Truth &Knowledge (Indigo Colour) associated with power of intuition & balanced state of mind	Nervous system, **Metaphysical Element- Mind & Intellect**	Ajna Chakra (Medulla plexus)	Forehead (Between two-eyebrows) Shape- like **Two petals of lotus**	Nervous Disorder, decaying of brain cells, headache migraine, meningitis, ophthalmic diseases, blindness, strain etc.
7. Bliss (Violet Colour) associated with absolute Peace & wisdom	Endocrine System, **Metaphysical Element- Cosmic Power**	Sahasrar Chakra (crown Chakra) or cerebral glandplexus	Top of head (Crown), Shape- **Thousand petals of lotus**	Hormonal deficiency, depression, confusion, apathy, dullness, low IQ, EQ & SQ etc.

AWARENESS OF SELF AND AURA

Awareness means understanding of inner as well as outer system of self & body. Physical body is the resultant of our inner body. *That is why a healthy life means heal thy life (inner body healing which means presence of all primary virtues or basic qualities for a life).*

Kirlan Camera can take photograph of inner body. Presence of all primary virtue creates a perfect aura around physical body, which serves as a shield to the physical body. There are continuous radiation of colours and vibration of our inner body through our thoughts, emotions and visualisation. Non-radiation of any colour of virtues creates a hole in the aura, which is shielding our physical body from bad affects of planets and stars. People use gems of different colours as a substitute of particular colours and vibration. But this is a temporary shield and its effect depends upon its reality in life style.

Waste and negative thoughts destroy the aura. Therefore planets and stars easily affect our physical and mental state. Thus we are ourselves responsible for our own course of action, direction and condition. This is the truth, which we need to be aware of.

Awareness of truth enlightens us and the darkness of ignorance gets vanished. This is what we pray to God "Tamso Ma Jyotirgamaya, Asado Ma Sadgamaya & Mrityo Ma Amritam Gamaya." When we move from darkness of ignorance to the light of knowledge, from untruth to truth and from mortality of physical body to immortality of our own inner subtle body, we get illuminated and become the perennial fountain of knowledge, Peace, Purity, Love, Happiness, Bliss & Powers.

Application of "Tilak" on forehead means awareness of self as a source of pure energy positioned at Agya chakra. It is internal and not external to show others.

Tying the "Thread" in right hand means tying mental body with right consciousness of primary virtues. This is also internal. External thread tied in right hand will neither purify mental energy nor protect physical body.

5

THOUGHT SYSTEM OF CONSCIOUS MIND
(The Emotional Self)

Conscious mind is one of the faculties of the soul, which receives and creates thoughts, desires, images, ideas, feelings and emotions. It receives the thoughts and emotions either from sense organ of the body (eyes, ears, nose, tongue and skin) or from internal faculties called subconscious or unconscious mind also known as memory bank.

So, the thoughts in conscious mind are the seeds of action and experience. When there is a thought of desire for pure experience, coupled with the realisation of the importance of quality of thought, then naturally those seeds will be selected which will bear the desired fruit. The desire may be for peace, knowledge, contentment, love, power, joy, insight or any one of the positive experiences may be savoured to feel those past happy moments from the subconscious mind and of course there will be the aim to control or eradicate those thoughts and impressions which are the seeds of disharmony and peacelessness.

Functions of the Conscious Mind

Thoughts, imaginations, creation of ideas, sensations, desire, feelings and emotions are essential functions of the emotional self. *The soul uses the conscious mind as a screen or field on which thoughts, desires, sensations and ideas are projected as images. An experience, feeling or emotions, of these images is the impact of these projections, which is also known as state of mind.*

If I want to feel good, I have to have the type of thoughts that bring the quality of goodness. **However, conscious mind is subject to the whims and inconsistencies of the intellect. Wherever the intellect roams, the conscious mind automatically follows, producing all of its essential functions.** The core beliefs described therein are based on the emotional needs of the 'inner child' (Active impressions in memory of a soul) and these determine how we will interact with others. Based on this need, we face people with openness and optimism, or with fear, despair, hatred, hostility etc.

Because of the unfulfilled need for safety, love or self-identity we tend to believe that we are unworthy of anything that would provide these. Then our thoughts, actions, and beliefs are in reaction to our core belief, either striving to counter its influences or succumbing to that belief. *In the face of an emotional need, our heart rules our head. Logic can neither sway, nor argue the 'inner child' into submission because our child's emotional needs far outweigh intellectual reasoning. The foundation of the emotional self is love that comes from within, assuring us that we are now safe and taken care of. When we clear away the painful, non-living beliefs and behaviours, the 'inner child' and ourselves open up for nurturance by God by divinising the intellect and filling the mind with positive emotions.*

TYPES OF THOUGHTS AND EMOTIONS RECEIVED BY CONSCIOUS MIND

Subconscious mind or memory bank is the store of all impressions of our experiences and actions, though we are not aware of them. They are latent. Human personality is adjusted by these latencies or potentials only. These latencies or hidden potentials can be compared to an iceberg. Hardly 10% of the iceberg is visible above the surface of the water. More than 90% of the iceberg is invisible beneath the water line. Therefore even powerful storm cannot change the direction of iceberg because of a strong undercurrents running in opposite direction of the powerful storm and controlling more than 90% of the iceberg. Similarly what we know about other's character or behaviour is only a tiny amount of the 10% visible. 90% of our invisible personality which is within the subconscious and unknown to even ourselves is controlled by some very strong undercurrents and is the driving force of our personality in a particular direction. This is called

ACTIVE *UNDERCURRENTS OR* **ACTIVE IMPRESSIONS** *OR ACTIVE SUB CONSCIOUS MEMORIES*, which are the records of small and big events of the recent past life or past events of this life since childhood, or impressions of previous birth, which influence our personality and keep moulding our character subconsciously.

Day to day impressions, which are recorded by our visualisation and associations, are also part of the active memory. And thus this active impressions (memory) work like an under current, which determine the direction of our present attitudes, belief, fears, prejudices and all subconscious behaviour. This is also called the inner child who is very arrogant and outweighs intellect appeals.

It is the subconscious memory which gives a man a unified character or personality from moment to moment in its normal state of wakefulness and these active impressions keep coming in our conscious mind in a form of thought energy, desires, feelings and emotions which is called consciousness which further determines our *state of mind, attitudes, visions and influences our decisions and actions which further strengthens that same impressions in our active memory which is called a strong belief* and this beliefs will be automatically reflected from time to time through our characters and behaviours.

Following are the **six types of thoughts and emotions** that keep coming to our conscious mind from active or inactive memories of our subconscious or unconscious mind **at the rate of more that 30 thoughts per minute.**

A. WASTE THOUGHTS

These thoughts are not related to any necessary or productive work. **Such thoughts may not release toxic chemicals yet waste time and energy.** These thoughts are mainly connected with the past happenings, events and upon which the conscious mind and intellect keeps on brooding. These thoughts even mix up with the thoughts coming from sense organ and create gloomy images about the unknown future or start day dreaming and making castles in the air. And frequent repetitions of these dreams create wrong belief and attitudes in life and lead to depression or frustration and create worry about the unknown future.

B. NEGATIVE THOUGHTS

These thoughts are related to disadvantages of various events and loss as being perceived by the individual. **Such thoughts increase toxic chemicals in our body.** These are the impressions in our active memories, which are related to low self-esteem, inferiority complex, weak impressions, vicious habits and tendencies, selfishness, anger, ego and attached blind emotions. These impressions with very negative emotions even compel us to act without any decision of intellect. These negative emotions of our memories are very powerful. They incapacitate the intellect by creating mental limits, false associated assumptions and prejudiced judgments and hasty or blind actions. For example:

i. If any mistakes happen, we often say, ' this is my nature, I can't help it, I have always been like that, I will not change now, it is too late... thus we make a limit and create a comfort zone with these unnatural tendencies, and these limits become a strong mental logical barrier in our Subconcious mind that makes it impossible for us to find the solution of a problem.

ii. There may be someone regularly cleaning the office, where we have a set of beautiful flower vases of glass.
By chance, he happens to break it. We caution him that he has to be careful otherwise must replace the same with another one if broken again. After a few days some thing happens as he was cleaning again and he breaks the another one. We become firm with him and tell him the next time if he breaks anything; he has to replace with another one from his own pocket. Some days later, we come in the office and as we pass by that place we find that the flower vase is broken and mended with some solutions. Now who would come in our memory that could have done that? Immediately we associate our previous memory and call the same person and take action

against him but actually it was not he, it was somebody else who had done that.

Thus we see here that our own negative thoughts and emotions led us to a prejudiced wrong judgement.

iii. There is one more story, which explains how our negative emotions lead us to blind deadly actions. There was a farmer who had a mongoose as pet. The farmer and his son with this pet used to live together. Pet was very lovely and faithful. All of them lived and slept together. One-day farmer went outside leaving his son and pet at home. Suddenly a cobra snake appeared and it was about to bite farmer's son. Suddenly the pet bounced and caught the snake and cut it into pieces. The pet fulfilled its loyalty to the farmer. Its mouth was full of blood. Farmer's son was afraid and had hidden himself in another room. When the farmer came back. The pet appeared before him proudly with more lovely emotions expecting same from the farmer in lieu of its loyalty. But farmer's conscious mind flooded with negative associated memories from subconscious mind and created strong negative emotions of hatred (thinking that the blood in the mouth of his pet was of his son and his son was no more and his pet had killed his only son in his absence) and at once raised the spade kept in corner of the room and killed this pet on the spot. After that his son appeared before him and by seeing his son he become dumb stuck. And when he listened the true story from his son about the pet, he became grief stricken and started burning mentally in the fire of agony and repentance.

Thus our own negative belief or impression makes us unfaithful, doubtful, resentful, weak and creates strong impressions of low self esteem in memory bank which further make our personality negative and thus a man is trapped in his own negative vicious cycle.

C. NECESSARY THOUGHT

There are strong impressions of repeated routine actions in our active memory or subconscious mind. These are the thoughts related to necessary activities and daily routine. Such thoughts cannot be avoided completely.

A desire in conscious mind for routine work or knowledge activates the memory by which necessary thoughts automatically occupy our conscious mind and intellect and activate motor organs of our body to perform the task. It is related to day-to-day routine work, professional job, career plans etc. For example the desire to go to office from home and back automatically activates our motor organs and all necessary turns are made automatically to reach the destination. Similarly a desire to type something activates stored necessary memory and fingers get automatic instructions from sub conscious mind to type the detail as far as it can. Thus our habits and tastes are part of necessary thoughts of our active memory or subconscious mind.

D. POSITIVE THOUGHTS

Thoughts related to success, health, peace, self-esteem, and direct or indirect advantages of every event are called positive thoughts. These are value-based thoughts, which have no selfish intentions, and we feel joy, peace, happiness and enthusiasm. These are not at fully active state. When these positive thoughts mix with thoughts and desires created by sense organs it creates a joyful and peaceful state of mind which further makes our attitudes very positive and creates a constructive vision and powerful actions which makes our impressions pure and positive in active memory. Thus positive thoughts generate energy and strength to cleanse further our active memory and get rid of negative and wasteful memories.

E. PURE THOUGHTS (THOUGHTS OF HIGHER CONSCIOUSNESS)

The thoughts, which replace impure thoughts (waste & negative thoughts) are called pure thoughts, which have the power to purify our own impressions of memories. **Constant generation of pure thoughts not only purifies our own latencies, habits & instincts but purifies others' nature also.** Pure thoughts are strong seeds of positive personality. They not only help an individual to become socially adaptable but empower him to become socially effective also. He thus plays a crucial role in a society to start a changing process. He becomes the centre of revolution for a pure and ultra modern civilization with peace, purity and prosperity, which becomes the root of all civilizations of the world.

F. ELEVATED AND POWERFUL THOUGHTS

Thoughts related to spirituality, yoga and self-consciousness are called elevated and powerful thoughts. **They reduce toxic chemicals from blood and increase health-promoting chemicals.** These are the most powerful seeds in human being's unconscious mind. When this seed is watered by powerful emotions, the tree of a divine personality starts germinating. When the tree grows, it becomes the living divine idol or perfect personality on this earth. Thus the powerful thoughts purify the whole nature. The powerful thoughts occur in the absence of all other thoughts. The third eye gets completely activated with the powerful thought. Power of silence flows all around and miracle starts happening. Individual reaches to the acne of spirituality. What science cannot do, spirituality does it. This is the state of "self " or "soul" consciousness.

THOUGHT: THE MOST POWERFUL SUBTLE ENERGY

A thought is the seed of all actions. It carries the most powerful subtle energy in potential form. It is just like uranium, which makes a nuclear bomb. When uranium disintegrates by chain reaction, the energy is released. In the same way when the thought is bombarded by emotions, it releases its massive energy as happens in the case of nuclear chain reaction. When a powerful seed of thought is bombarded by powerful emotions, a strong vibration is created into the universe. Waste and negative thoughts are just like a nuclear waste, which create hazard in the Eco system.

EMOTIONS: THE FORCE THAT DIRECTS THOUGHT ENERGY

Emotions give motion to thoughts' energy. It makes thoughts to move in the direction where emotions carry it further. It makes the being (soul) emotional by which course of actions or reactions are determinated. Emotion is the force of determination too. That is why a person is carried away by his emotions. It is also the marks that fit over deep true self and obscure us from ourselves.

Without emotion, thought is mechanical. Emotion makes the thought magnetic. *Without emotion, thoughts can be compared to an engine running vehicle in a neutral gear. Emotion changes the gears of thoughts, which makes the vehicle of thought to move*

Emotion can also be compared to involvement of heart and soul. Thought with emotion indicates involvement of mind's coordination with heart.

Thus emotion is the "Essence" or the prime source of motivation of the "Being". Performances and artwork were created with emotional energy only.

It can be easily understood by an example. Simply chanting mantra during prayer does not give peace of mind because it is mechanical at thought level. Prayer with divine emotions is called devotion. And devotion gives complete peace of mind, which activates our magnetic center that further creates effective and serene vibrations in the atmosphere.

Understanding one's own and others' emotions and taking empathetic view is called **"Emotional intelligence"**

TYPES OF EMOTIONS

Emotions may be categorised as follow:

A. Positive Emotions: Those emotions which create a positive state of mind and fill the mind with pure love, peace, bliss, joy and happiness etc. Following emotions are categorised as positive:

- pure love (true love)
- compassion
- peace or equanimity

- divine love (devotions) etc.
- laughter or mirth
- awe or wonder

B. Negative Emotions: Negative emotions are afflictive and damaging to our goal of emotional harmony. These emotions fill the state of mind with fear, disgust, apprehension, anger, sex lust; pride etc. which further lead to depression and pessimistic attitude in life. Following emotions are categorised as negative emotions:

- erotic love or sex lust
- fear
- revulsion or disgust
- anger etc.

C. Powerful Emotions: (Emotion of Valour and Heroism): Powerful emotion of valour and heroism fill our mind with courage and dynamism. They enable the modern day *Arjunas* to live their lives as **INTEGRATED BEINGS**, and who don't allow its pressures and strains to fragment them. They mature into beings who, instead of running away, seek out their inner demons and dragons and face them bravely. They know they cannot control circumstances, but only responsed to them, and they go ahead and do precisely that. They don't let odds bog them down but seek out the courage, inner resources, and skills to advise, again and again, from the ashes of their old selves.

Thus the powerful emotions not only fill the mind with confidence and determination but germinate the powerful seed of thought also to rediscover the self with a perfect personality which becomes a catalyst agent for world transformation through self-transformation.

6

EFFECTS OF THOUGHTS AND EMOTIONS ON STATE OF MIND AND BODY

Any thought in conscious mind triggers respective emotional memory (Good or Bad) which in turn fills the mind with respective emotions (Positive, negative or powerful), which further creates the respective attitude (positive or negative) which in turn triggers the intellect's vision to take respective decisions for actions which further creates, recreates or strengthens the impressions in our memory bank (Sub-conscious mind), and these impressions stimulate the sensations (feeling) in our body by activating our endocrine glands. Thus any thought would follow the following path to affect our mind and body:

THOUGHTS >> EMOTIONS (FROM EMOTIONAL MEMORY) >> ATTITUDE >> VISIONS >> DECISIONS >> ACTIONS (BY BODY) >> IMPRESSIONS (IN MEMORY) >> SENSATION (FEELING IN BODY) OR REFLECTIONS >> ACTIVATION OF GLANDS AND RELEASING HORMONES >> BODY GETS AFFECTED

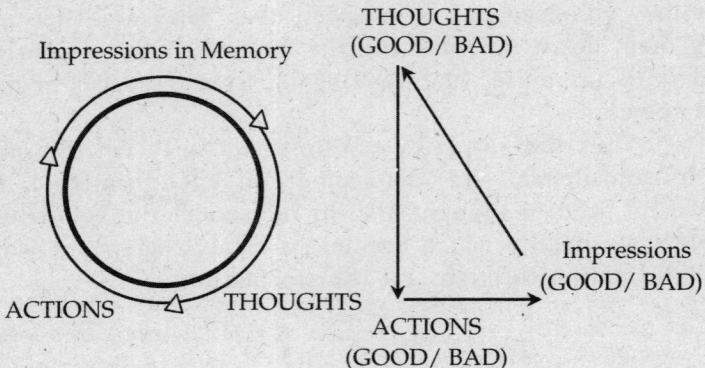

Impressions in Memory

ACTIONS — THOUGHTS

THOUGHTS (GOOD/ BAD)

ACTIONS (GOOD/ BAD)

Impressions (GOOD/ BAD)

TEAM OF CONSCIOUS MIND

T- Thoughts
E- Emotions
A- Attitude
M- Memories

Thoughts: It is the input in our conscious mird which either comes from perception by sense organs or automatically keeps coming from memory bank (From subconscious or unconscious mind).

Emotions: When thoughts come from memories.they also carry emotions with it, which is also called **"emotional memory"**.

Thus we can say that *Emotional memory* is the memory attached to emotion in conjunction with past events, people and places. For example: you are driving a car with music on, suddenly any accident happens. Now this gets recorded in memory bank attached to the emotions or feelings while listening to that particular music during driving the car. Now whenever you will listen that particular music, you will get the whole picture of the accident scene and your emotions will shift automatically.

The memory here indicates mental visual imagery (just like videotape or video CD, or DVD) of our past lives or past actions, reactions etc. It also contains some future planned images which are created by individual visualizations or we can say it is the imaginary world of the individual in which he expects or plans to live in. This is also known as *"unreal memory"*. When this file is opened in conscious mind, individual gets lost in wild world of fantasies or imaginations. **Thus our memory bank contains real as well as unreal memories.**

ATTITUDE: THOUGHT + EMOTIONS

When thought and emotions meet together, attitudes are created. Positive thoughts with positive emotions create positive attitude, negative thoughts with negative emotions create negative attitude. Thoughts without emotions create neutral attitude. A person with neutral attitude becomes sloth, careless and charmless.

In laymen language "Attitude can be described as intensity of emotion with thoughts" or "attitude indicates the magnitude of emotions with thoughts." In a more simple way it can be compared with an example: simple thought indicates a vehicle standing in the neutral gear of a running engine and attitude accelerates the vehicle by changing the gears (mode of mind).

Memories: Brain processing or memory accessing can be compared to separate filing cabinets:

A. Negative emotions record in memory bank
B. Positive emotions record in memory bank

AS ARE THE MEMORIES SO IS THE CONSCIOUSNESS.

TEAM: — *"Team" indicates Thought + Emotions+ Attitude+ Memory* together forming thoughts in our consciousness or in conscious mind.

The term "consciousness" indicates here the memory-linked thoughts with emotional memory, which fills the state of mind with emotions which is called emotional state of mind and further determines our attitude in particular situation or circumstances.

Thus the" TEAM" of conscious mind further determines the course of intellect (the third eye). As the "attitude "so is the "vision" of third eye. As the "vision", so is the "decision" and "action". As the "action" so is the "strengthening" of "impressions" in the memories. And as the "impressions" so is the "sensation" or feeling or "realization".

Example: The recollection of consciousness of a dog having once bitten someone now fills the mind with the state of fear and attitude or mood (mode of mind) of aversion. He views the dog as an enemy and acts with a stick. This in turn strengthens the impression of fear from a dog in his sub conscious mind (memory). Thus the feelings of a man depend upon what he is conscious of. This team will further affect our body.

HOW DO OUR MIND AND BODY GET AFFECTED BY TEAM

EFFECTS OF BAD TEAM:

ON MIND:
Bad Thoughts à Negative Emotions >> Negative Attitude >>
Imperfect visions (misconceptions) >> Wrong decisions >>
Hasty Actions >> Bad Impressions >> Feelings of depression
>> Mind Becomes Un-eased (Dis-eased) by anger, agitation
and excitement etc.

ON BODY:
BY ANGER: Releases bad cholesterol LDL – (low density lipo
proteins) >> Blocks heart vessels >> Blood pressure rises
leading to heart attacks and intestines get wounded causing
ulcers, etc.

BY AGITATION: Increases the activity of the sympathetic
nervous system >> Increases pressure in the small blood
vessels of the brain >> Brain vessels are ruptured leading
either to brain hemorrhage or brain tumour/cancer.

BY EXCITEMENT AND FEAR: Activates adrenal glands >>
Negative harmones (adrenaline/cortisol) released >> Causes
many disorders or disease in body organs such as diabetes,
kidney failure, skin disease etc.

THUS A DIS–EASED TEAM LEADS TO A DISEASED BODY

THOUGHT ATTACK LEADS TO HEART ATTACK
Thus by above chain reaction of thoughts, it is quiet obvious
that a waste or negative thought can lead to heart attack.
Thus the thought attacks are more deadly than heart attacks.
It not only causes heart attack by paralysing the whole inner
system of being but also paralyses our body.

EFFECTS OF GOOD TEAM ON MIND
Good thoughts (positive, elevated and powerful thoughts)
>> Positive emotions >> Positive attitude >> Creative and

constructive vision of intellect >> Effective decision >> Successful action >> Remarkable impressions in memory >> True realization (feeling) of our own potential >> Thrilling and happy sensation in body >> Stability or easiness in mind which further makes our body healthy.

EFFECTS OF GOOD TEAM ON BODY

1. Creates balance between sympathetic and parasympathetic system, between steroid hormones and lactic acid, stabilises blood pressure to the necessary level and so on >> Healthy mind and receptive mind in a well nourished brain for better memory

2. Releases endorphin and encephalin hormones >> Gives relaxation to 60 trillions of cells in human body >> Human system and organs remain healthy and disease free.

3. Releases HDL (High density lipo protein) i.e. good cholesterol >> Replaces bad cholesterol >> Blockage clearing of heart vessels >> Makes our heart filled with pure love and positive emotions >> Rules out chances of heart attacks.

Thus a healthy TEAM leads to healthy body (a better place for being- The soul to live in)

HOW A GOOD TEAM LEADS TO SUCCESS

When we think positive in a happy and confident frame of mind, we easily get access to our sub conscious impressions of successful experiences while presented with the problems. With a positive mood, we can recall all the successful solutions to the similar problems of the past, thus increasing our chances of a successful solution.

When we are linked to impressions of negative emotions while facing a problem, our search for solution from our memory becomes a futile exercise because we keep accessing failure memories only from our experiences of past.

HOW TO SWITCH OVER FROM BAD TEAM TO A GOOD TEAM

To switch over from bad team to good team we have to create our own magic trigger. So select a magic trigger from the past successful memories. It has to be selected and practiced well in advance. It cannot be set up when we are already in our negative mood due to our own bad team. Thus the magic trigger becomes a permanent key of positive experience.

Now whenever you are in a sad or depressed mood due to your bad team, take the following five steps:

Step I: Recall the Magic Trigger,

Step II: Recall the scene of magic trigger in complete detail,

Step III: Feel the same emotions while replaying the actual event in detail,

Step IV: Now experience the change of mood and remain for some time in the same feeling and experience,

Step V: Now challenge the problem being faced and search for solution. You will certainly find it.

7

MIND AND BRAIN RELATIONSHIP

When Albert Einstein died, his brain was brought in a laboratory and was examined meticulously and was compared with a common man's brain. On comparison it was found that there existed no dissimilarities of even .001 %. Both the brains were exactly similar. Then what made Albert Einstein's brain so special? It was the Einstein being's mind which utilised more than 10 % of his brain's trillions of neurons.

Here mind means metaphysical or subtle body, which uses physical brain either for logic, reasoning, and analysis or for art and creativity.

The human brain is a paired organ; it is composed of two halves, called cerebral hemisphere. The theory of the structure and functions of the mind suggests that the two sides of the brain control two different modes of thinking.

Just stop to wonder for a moment how a two year old baby can master the task of speaking so effortlessly while most adult efforts at learning a foreign language tend to end up as more effort and less learning. Most children are born with right hemisphere dominant, when an infant learns a language; she does so with all her senses of smell, sounds, colours, feelings in the learning process. As we grow older, the left hemisphere modes of thinking which rely heavily on partial processes (without visualisations) of the intellect – logic, sequence, organization- become dominant.

In the Zen tradition the left mind is associated with the process of thinking and the right mind is associated with knowing. Most individuals tend to have a distinct preference for one or the other side of the brain. From very early in life, school and society too conspire to identify individual as the one or the other – Arts or the Science and label them as "Creative or logical"

Mind uses left hemisphere of brain for logical and verbal reasoning. It deals with words, analysis (breaking a part) and sequential thinking.

Mind uses right hemisphere of brain for intuition, creativity, dealing with pictures, synthesis (putting together) and holistic thinking.

Brain itself does not do anything. In the absence of mind (conscious life force) brain is called dead.

Right hemisphere of brain is mostly used by intellect's creative and visualisation power (third eye)

DIFFERENCE BETWEEN MIND AND BRAIN

MIND	BRAIN
METAPHYSICAL (FACULTY OF SOUL)	PHYSICAL (PART OF BODY)
MIND'S THOUGHTS ARE LIKE SOFTWARE.	IT IS LIKE HARDWARE OF COMPUTER.
THREE FACULTIES (MIND, INTELLECT & IMPRESSIONS)	TWO PARTS OF BRAIN(LEFT AND RIGHT)
	LEFT IS USED FOR ANALYSIS.
	RIGHT IS USED FOR CREATIVITY.

THOUGHT AND EMOTIONS OF MIND (Subconscious, Conscious and Intellect) CREATE CYCLES OF WAVES IN THE BRAIN, WHICH ARE CALLED "BRAIN WAVES" AND THESE BRAIN WAVES ARE MEASURED BY ELECTRO ENCEPHALO GRAM (EEG)

TYPES OF BRAIN WAVES

Thought is an energy, which is created in conscicus mind by the input of either sense organs or memories. When thoughts enter into the brain, brain waves are created. Thoughts can be compared to stones or pebbles and brain can be compared to a pond. When pebbles or stones of thoughts are thrown into the pond of brain, ripples in the brain are created. Thoughts are also similar to electrical

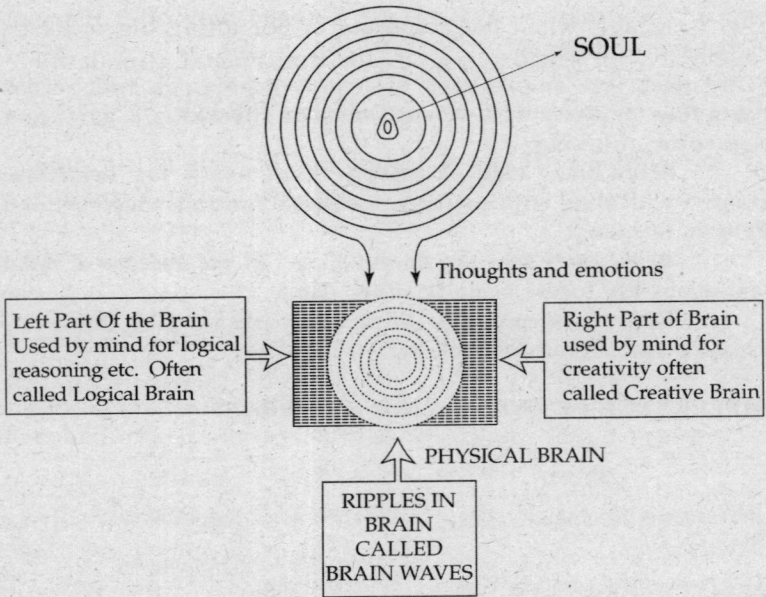

current. When an electrical current enters into a wire, a wave of frequency 50hz is created in the wire. These waves are categorised as per their frequency and voltage. These are:

(a) ALPHA WAVES: These are moderately fast (8 to 13 cycles per sec) and are relatively high voltage waves. Normally, EEG records these waves when an individual is awake, has his eyes closed and is in a relaxed state and his cerebrum is idling so to say. It keeps our mind and body in relaxed and receptive state. It is having a vast potential for performance. Alpha state of mind triggers our standard impressions of memory.

(b) BETA WAVES: These are comparatively faster (13 to 25 cycles per sec) than alpha waves but in amplitude they are lower in voltage. Beta waves are obtained when an individual is awake, has his eyes open, and is in an activated or attentive state, that is to say, when his cerebrum is not idling but is busily engaged with sensory stimulation and menta stimulation.

Beta waves are further categorised as follows:

(1) Normal Range: Between 13 and 18 Hz. This is triggered by routine impressions. In this state we are busy and active. **Biochemistry, hormones and enzymes levels remains within normal range.** Continuing in beta waves gives tiredness signal to subconscious mind.

(2) Abnormal Range (β+): Between 18 and 25 Hz. Thoughts of waste impressions of our memory bank trigger these waves. **Biochemistry and secretion of hormones and enzymes get affected.** Tiredness and stress increases. Disturbance in easiness of mind causes diseases in body.

(3) Most Abnormal Range (Super β) - Between 25 and 50 Hz. Thoughts of negative impressions of our memory bank trigger these waves and further cause distress and depressions in life. **All types of diseases start, immune system gets weakened. Brain cells and capillaries get ruptured which further cause brain hemorrhage and paralysis.**

(4) Deranged Range Beyond 50hz – Sign of mental disorder and madness. It also indicates loss of memory.

(c) THETA WAVES: These are moderately slow (3 to 7cycles per sec) and low voltage waves that predominate when drowsiness descends. This is a dream state. Consciousness never functions but intellect keeps functioning with uncontrolled visualisation of images from subconscious mind. All randomly recorded images (Recorded by electronic or print media and by visualisations of waste and negative images during awake state) get opened during dream state, which makes our brain to work during sleep. This lowers the potential and creates a low voltage. This further gives tiredness despite sleeping more.

(d) DELTA WAVES: These are the lowest (0.5 to 3 cycles per sec) brain waves and they have a high voltage. They are recorded when an individual is in deep sleep. Because of this fact, the physiologists refer to deep sleep as Slow Wave Sleep (SWS). This is the deep state of sleep that gives complete relaxation to our mind, intellect and body. Our mind and body get charged due to deep relaxation. Constant state of delta waves triggers our standard impressions, which renew us physically, mentally and spiritually. All inventions take place during this concentrated state of mind. **Mystery of universe sometimes gets revealed during dream waves between 3.5 to 4 Hz.**

If the EEG indicates that the cerebrum is producing no brain waves, it is called a flat EEG and is considered to imply that the individual is dead.

These brain waves can also be understood by following examples:(See Figure on page 42)

Brain is just like a pond, where water is still and one can see one's face very clearly as there are no ripples on the surface of water. Thoughts and emotions can be compared to pebbles and stones, when these pebbles and stones are thrown into the pond there are several ripples created on the surface of water due to agitations caused by stones. Similarly, when pebbles and stones of thoughts and emotions from our metaphysical mind enter into the pond of physical brain, agitations into the brain are caused and different types of brain waves are created depending upon the nature of (size of) pebbles and stones of thoughts and emotions from mind entering into the brain. One cycle in one second is called one Hz.

1Cycle per second = 1 HZ

(FREQUENCY OF BRAIN IS MEASURED IN HERTZ.)

THOUGHTS, BRAIN WAVES AND BODY RELATIONSHIP

Thoughts of our mind create waves in our brain. These brain waves affect our endocrine system, which further change biochemistry of our body. Following table explains it in a simple way.

TABLE SHOWING THOUGHTS, BRAIN WAVES AND BODY RELATIONSHIP

Types Of Thoughts	Comparison of size with pebbles or stones	Waves created by Brain by Thoughts & Voltage	Effects of Thoughts on Body
Negative	Very Big Stone	Very high Beta Waves (> than 25 Htz.) & very low Voltage. Since energy comes out rapidly from body.	Distress state which causes raise in BP & secretion of Adrenaline & Cortisol harmone & biochemistry of body is derailed & state of mind is fully disturbed.
Waste	Big Stones	High Beta waves. (more than 18 Htz.) Low Voltage because energy comes out due to repeated thinking.	Stressful state of mind, Anxiety, fear, depression & Frustration. Low energy level, biochemistry of body disturbed. Digestive system & endocrine system suffers.
Necessary	Small Stones	Beta waves.(up to 18 Htz.) & low voltage.	Normal state but apprehensive,hasty decision & Action, feels tired often.
Positive	Small Pebbles	Alpha Waves & High Voltage	Relaxed state of mind, Energetic, high voltage, Dynamic state within. Ready to face any challenges in life, Secretion of endorphin & encephalin gives relaxation to whole body.
Dream stage (Random recorded thoughts coming from intellect automatically for imgination)	Small pebbles & stones	Theta waves & low voltage because energy comes out of body during imagination in the dreams.	Feels the reality as per imagination in dreams & body reacts as it reacts during awake. i.e. Horror dream activates horror syndromes and body reacts accordingly.
Deep Sleep State	Smallest pebbles	Delta waves (Delta Waves) & very high voltage energy remain present in the body	Completely relaxed state of mind as well as body. Balanced secretion of hormones & digestive juices. Full relaxation & very high degree of potential energy.

Extreme negative thoughts cause deranged range of brain waves beyond 50hz,which is a sign of mental disorder and madness. It also indicates loss of memory.

8

SOUL, MIND, AND BRAIN RELATIONSHIP

Hypothalamus is that part of the brain which through the pituitary gland controls all the endocrine glands and the secretion of harmones and it also controls the state of awakening and sleep in conjunction with the RAS (Reticular Activating System) and acts for expression or inhibition of emotions in co-ordination with the thalamus and the limbic system and works for sense perception and other mental actions.

SEATED HERE ON A THRONE LOCATED AT A PLACE BETWEEN THE TWO EYEBROWS THE SOUL ACTS THROUGH THE MECHANISM OF THE BRAIN AND THE BODY.

The schematic drawing on next page shows the inter action of the mind and body and the sequence of stimulus and response.

Some neuro-scientists say that there is time-lapse of a couple of seconds (or even a split second) between the sensory message perceived (stage 4) and the triggering of the action (stage 6) onwards and thus we can conclude that at stage 5 the decision to do or not to do or how and when to do is taken and therefore this is what explains the existence of soul here.

This is the place of "AKAL TAKHT" from where the timeless soul rules the metropolitan city; called 'the body' it is the window from which the soul sees the world. It is the safety valve or the casket in which soul, the greatest of all treasures lies. Soul is the highest executive running and organizing the most complex system known.

Though the soul is not a spatio-temporal entity and being infinitesimal, need not be pin-pointed in the brain, yet by indicating the place of its interaction with body mechanism

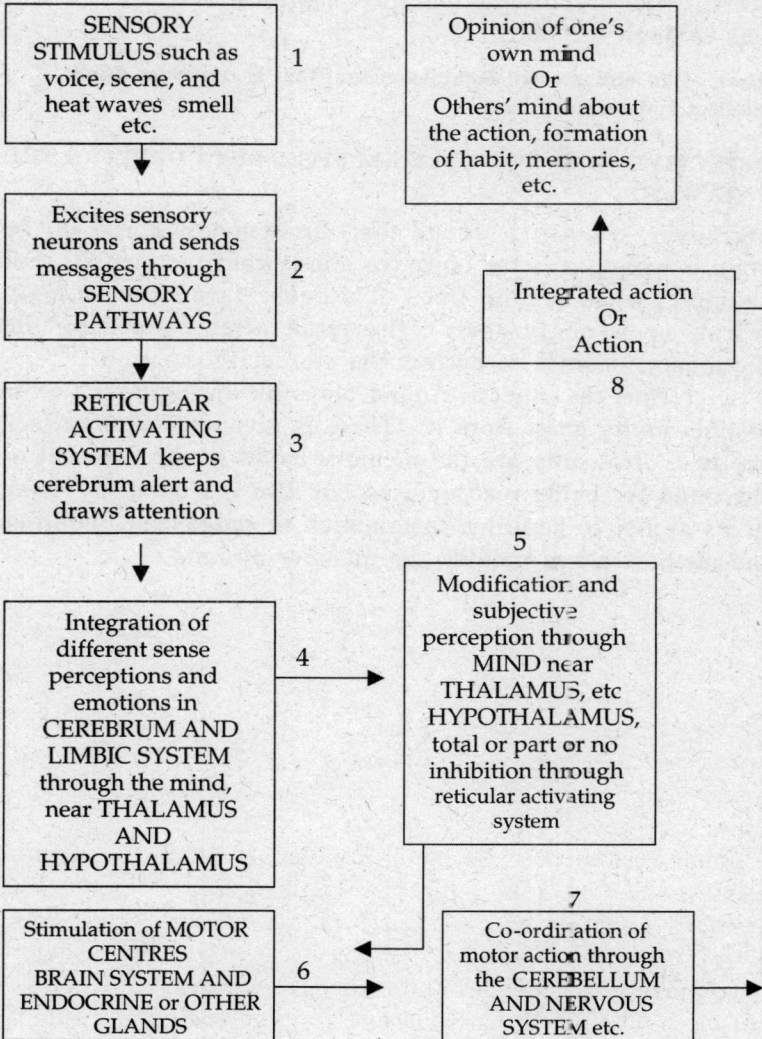

How soul acts through the mind and the body?

1 SENSORY STIMULUS such as voice, scene, and heat waves smell etc.		**9** Opinion of one's own mind Or Others' mind about the action, formation of habit, memories, etc.
↓		↑
2 Excites sensory neurons and sends messages through SENSORY PATHWAYS		**8** Integrated action Or Action
↓		
3 RETICULAR ACTIVATING SYSTEM keeps cerebrum alert and draws attention		
↓		**5** Modification and subjective perception through MIND near THALAMUS, etc HYPOTHALAMUS, total or part or no inhibition through reticular activating system
4 Integration of different sense perceptions and emotions in CEREBRUM AND LIMBIC SYSTEM through the mind, near THALAMUS AND HYPOTHALAMUS	→	
6 Stimulation of MOTOR CENTRES BRAIN SYSTEM AND ENDOCRINE or OTHER GLANDS		**7** Co-ordination of motor action through the CEREBELLUM AND NERVOUS SYSTEM etc.

we can show that the soul exists, that the soul is not identical
with or omnipresent in the body but it acts through a control
system and that it is not located in the heart muscle but in the
heart of the brain which controls heartbeat and from here it
acts through the body.

(Here Mind indicates all faculties of soul that is conscious mind,
intellect and memory bank)

OBJECTIVE MIND NOT ONLY RECEIVES BUT CORRECTS THE DATA ALSO

Moreover, when it is found that the memory stored in the
brain is wrong, it is the objective mind, which corrects it. For
example, when certain lines of a poem have been wrongly
learnt, or wrongly spelt , the mind after consulting the
dictionary, decides to correct the stored information.

Thus the objective mind plays on the brain, which is
another entity apart from it. There is give and take between
the two. Not only are the memory banks at the disposal of
the mind for being read or used but also the mind, by using
of its ability or scrutiny, imagination or judgement, modifies
the memories and moulds the memory-circuits.

9

CONTROL SYSTEM BY THIRD EYE
THE RATIONAL SELF

The faculty by which the soul can select its desired thoughts and emotions is **INTELLECT**, which is also known as third eye or divine eye or the rational self. The expressions "will power" is often used to refer to our ability to put our ideals into practice. We know our well being and resist activity, which is harmful. This is directly related to soul's intellectual strength. When we speak of weakness or strength in the soul, we are referring to the intellect. In the case of a weak soul it is almost as if the intellect plays no part in determining which thoughts arise in the mind, but come as if pushed by the impressions of subconscious mind or are triggered by the atmosphere around or the moods of others. On the contrary, a powerful soul enjoys the experience of its own choice regardless of external stimuli.

THUS, INTELLECT PERFORMS THREE FUNCTIONS:

(a) **Analyse** or discern or discriminate

(b) **Visualise** the several images related to the selected thoughts

(c) **Judges** or decides.

In other words, we can say that the intellect is gifted by soul with three powers:

(A) Power to **Discriminate**

(B) Power to **Visualise**

(C) Power to **Judge**

"THIRD EYE IS THE KEY OF MEMORY BANK"

II. KEY FUNCTIONS OF THE INTELLECT

Out of these three powers, **power to visualise** is the most important function of the intellect. **That is why, intellect is also 'third eye' or 'eye' of knowledge and this is the eye of soul.**

Decision making, discernment or discrimination power, reasoning power, ability to remember, associate and identify, will power, ability to understand, know and recognise, judgement etc. are **key functions of the rational self.**

Intellect, being the ruler of the mind, is the principal faculty of the soul. The feeble and befuddled intellect subjugates itself to two worlds: one is the eternal world of senses, and the other is the internal world of thoughts, feelings and personal traits. Intellect allows or refuses entry of thoughts into the process of action and result according to its own set of rules and perceptions that constitute our belief system which in turn control our attitudes. The accuracy of the role of intellect as doorkeeper can be heightened through meditation so that positive qualities are permitted while negative ones are weakened and transformed. The strengths or weaknesses of an individual depend upon how efficiently the intellect functions.

Some impressions are active, some are latent and some are inactive. **The third eye activates the latent and inactive impressions through the power of visualisation.**

III. METHODS OF VISUALISATION BY THIRD EYE TO PROGRAMME OUR SUBCONSCIOUS MIND (MEMORY BANK)

II.1. MENTAL MOVIE METHOD

This is one of the best methods of visualisation for sub-conscious mind programming. Follow the following steps:

a. Relax yourself and sit down comfortably as you sit down to watch a movie in a theatre.

b. Immobilise your attention. Withdraw yourself from sensory perception. Feel happy that you are going to see the best movie of your choice.

c. Visualise a screen in front of you. Start making colourful mental pictures systematically and not randomly. It is better to form a systematic blue print of your mental movie.

d. During visualisation feel the true emotions as it is happening in real. Concentrate with all sensory perception that you are listening to the talks and feeling it very real and you are extremely happy for realizing your goal in your life. You must act as if this is already an objective reality.

e. Remain in happy mood and feel you are repeating this story to your friends, parents etc and listening their voices and feeling excited and going to sleep. Your memory is programmed now. Wait patiently and start the systematic work as per your blue print and see the success is being realised without any hindrances.

RECOVERY OF A PATIENT FROM PARALYSIS

A patient suffering from functional paralysis used to visualise a vivid picture (like movie) of himself walking around in his office, touching the desk, answering the telephone and doing all the things he ordinarily would do if he were healed. He repeated these visualisations exercise daily. By doing so he programmed his memory with the impression of perfect health. He continued this visualization regularly. Then, one day the telephone rang at a time when everyone else was away. The telephone, was then a few feet away from his bed, nevertheless, he manages to answer it. His paralysis vanished from that hour on. **The healing power of his memory bank had responded to his third eye imagery, and a healing followed.**
This man had suffered from a mental block that prevented nerve impulses generated in the brain from reaching his legs. Therefore, he could not walk. When he shifted his attention to the healing power within, his power flowed through his focussed attention and he could walk again.

II.2. ALPHA MIND TECHNIQUE

Alpha mind means relaxed state of mind when there is absence of Beta activities in the brain waves. Brain waves remain in Alpha pattern with a frequency between 8 to 12 cycles per second (Hz). In this state the negative thoughts, which tend to neutralize our desire and so prevent acceptance by our sub conscious mind, are no longer present.

Alpha state of mind occurs during a drowsy state or sleepy state and after you have just woke up. Alpha state of mind can also be created by deep contemplation, relaxation techniques and meditation.

In alpha mind techniques a person visualises his suggestion, which easily gets impressed in our memory bank because our subconscious mind remains quite receptive due to absence of any conscious efforts or activities.

Suppose you want to get rid of a destructive habit. Assume a comfortable posture, relax your body, and be still. Slowly you will feel going into a sleepy state. During that time say quietly over and over, "I am completely free from my bad and destructive habits. I am a peaceful soul, I am a pure soul." Repeat these words slowly, quietly and lovingly with true feelings daily before going to bed and just after waking up in the morning. Each time with repetition the emotional value becomes greater. And later on when the urge comes to repeat the negative habit repeat this formula out loud to yourself. Say, I am a pure soul. By this means you induce the memory bank to accept the idea and a healing follows. And efficacy of control system improves.

II.3. THE AFFIRMATIVE PRAYER METHOD

To affirm is to state that it is so as you maintain this attitude of mind as true, regardless of all evidence to the contrary. You will receive an answer to your prayer. Your thoughts can only affirm, for even if you deny something. You are actually affirming the presence of what you deny. Repeating an affirmation, knowing what you are saying and why you are saying it, lead the mind to that state of consciousness where it accepts what you state as true.

Keep on affirming the truths of life until you get the subconscious reaction that satisfies   Never give up affirmation till you get the desired result.

The effectiveness of an affirmation is determined largely by our understanding of the truth and meaning that underlie the words. The power of our affirmation lies in the intelligent application of definite and specific positive thoughts. Suppose a school child adds two and three and puts down four on the blackboard. The teacher affirms with mathematical certainty that two and three are five. Therefore, the child changes the figure accordingly. The teacher's statement did not make two plus three equal to five. This was already a mathematical truth. That in turn caused the child to rearrange the figure on the black board.

The result of the affirmative process of prayer depends on conforming to the principles of life, regardless of appearances. There is a principle of truth but none of dishonesty. There is a principle of intelligence but none of ignorance, there is a principle of health but none of disease and there is a principle of harmony and none of discord, and there is a principle of abundance and none of poverty.

Thus to affirm is to accept something as true, to live in the state of being it. As we sustain this mood, we shall experience the joy of the answered prayer. Successful prayer requires following basic steps:

a.   Acknowledge and admit the problem.

b.   Drop the problem into the memory bank, which alone knows the most effective solution or way out by third eye.

c.   Rest with a sense of deep conviction that it is done, visualise it confidently by your third eye.

These steps will enable the kinetic energy behind the prayer to takeover.

II.4. LOGICAL METHOD

This method consists of spiritual reasoning. You have to convince yourself that the instability of mind, stresses in your mind or sickness are the result of false beliefs, groundless fears and negative pattern of impressions in the memories. You have to reason it out clearly in your mind and convince that the diseases or ailments are due to only distorted and twisted patterns of thought that has taken form in the body. This wrong belief in some external power and external causes has now externalised itself as sickness and can be changed by changing the thought patterns.

In this method, you explain logically to yourself or the sick person that the basis of all healing is a change of belief. You must convince him that healing powers are hidden in the memory bank. You have to logically argue through your intellect in the courtroom of your objective mind that disease is a shadow of the mind, which is based on disease soaked in morbid thought imagery . Memory bank has an impression of a perfect pattern of every cell, nerve, and tissue within it.

Then, you must render a verdict or judgement through your intellect in the courthouse of your mind in favour of yourself and your patient. You liberate the sick one by strong faith, firm belief and spiritual understandings. Your mental and spiritual evidence is overwhelming. Since there are hidden impressions, what you feel as true is manifested in the experience of yourself or the patient, and healing follows automatically.

II.5. RAJYOGA METHOD

Many people throughout the world practise this form of treatment with wonderful results. I personally practised it during my treatment of cancer, diabetes and hepatitis-C. This method can be used to heal self and others too.

In this method, you visualise yourself in your true form, you slowly shift yourself into soul consciousness, after that you silently think of God and His qualities and attributes, such as god is blissful, ocean of love, infinitely intelligent, all powerful, a source of boundless wisdom, absolute harmony, indescribable beauty, and perfection. You quietly think and visualise along this lines, your consciousness is lifted into a new spiritual dimension. Your memory bank is opened. You get connected to the infinite intelligence. You feel the infinite ocean of God's love dissolving everything unlike itself in the mind and body.

You feel all the power and love of God are now focused on you and especially on the diseased organ of the body. Whatever is bothersome or vexing is now completely neutralised in the presence of the infinite ocean of love. Try to remain in this state of mind for quite some time. Healing has to follow, there is no doubt in it. After this you feel becoming completely all right and healthy.

You can heal others by this method also. You can visualise the patient and his diseased organ during this Rajyoga exercise. This method might be compared to the latest development in ultrasound, which generates powerful sound waves at extremely high frequencies. When these waves are focused on areas of the body where there are abnormal tissues, the affected cells resonate to the ultrasound and respond to it.

Similarly, to the degree, that we rise in consciousness by contemplating the qualities and attributes of God, we generate spiritual waves of harmony, health and peace. Those on whom these waves are focused, they resonate to them and respond. Many remarkable healings have been achieved by this technique of Rajyoga.

Additional chief of Brahma Kumaris Dadi Janki practises this meditation and is a living example for all of us. She remains in delta stage of mind all the time, she has been described as "The most stable mind in the world" by the scientists at the university of Texas, America and "A woman of perfect rhythm" by Australian scientists. She generates strong spiritual waves of health, harmony and peace all the times and serves the world indirectly.

II.6. BLESSING METHOD

A person who has practised Rajyoga for quite sometime can practise this method. Spiritual power goes into the world according to the feeling and faith behind it. When a Rajyogi realises the power, which moves the world, is moving on spirit's behalf and is backing the word uttered mentally, his confidence and assurance grow. You do not try to add power to power. There must be no mental striving, coercion, force, or mental wrestling. You just visualise the decree strongly that goes with boundless love, and infinite power, which brings the decree to be realised. Thus what you bless and feel as true will come to pass. Keep blessing the world with health, harmony peace and abundance of love indirectly. This is the incognito part you can play for serving the world. You can become a saint by using this method.

IV. WHY OUR DESIRES ARE NOT FULFILLED

Doubts and hesitation only weaken our prayer. Don't say to yourself, "I wish I could be healed " or 'I hope this works'. Our feeling about the work to be done sets the tone. Harmony is ours and health is ours.

When our desires in conscious mind and visualisation by third eye are in conflict, our visualisation invariably gains the way.

Suppose you were asked to walk along a narrow plank that was resting on the floor. You would do it easily, without question. But now suppose the same plank were twenty feet up, stretching between these walls, would you walk it? You would probably not. Your desire to walk the length of the plank would come into conflict with your visualisation. You would visualise yourself toppling off the plank and falling along way to the ground. You might very much want to walk across the plank, but your fear of falling would keep you away from being able to do it. The more effort you put into conquering your visualisation or suppressing it through your desire, the greater strength is given to the dominant visual imagery of falling.

Mental effort often leads to self-defeat, creating the opposite of what is desired. It is like deciding that you will do everything not to think of a black monkey. The decision makes the idea of a black monkey dominate the mind and our memory bank always responds more to the dominant idea. It will accept the stronger of two contradictory propositions. May be you find yourself thinking:

- I want a healing, why can't I get it?
- I try so hard, why don't I get the result?
- I must force myself to pray harder

Now you can realise where the error lies for the failure in fulfillment of your desires or prayers.

These all are due to mental pressures. Mental pressures raise your brain's beta activities and the door of memory bank gets automatically locked. And no idea can enter into your subconscious mind. Reflect on following example:

Have you ever had something like this happen to you? You have to take an examination of some kind. You have put in a lot of time studying and reviewing the material. You feel as if you know it well. But when you face a blank exam page due to not knowing certain question's answer, you find that your mind is even blanker. All your knowledge of the subject has suddenly deserted you. You can't recall a single relevant thought. You grit your teeth and summon all the power of your will but the harder you try, the farther the knowledge seems to flee.

All this happens due to rise in beta brain activities because of mental pressure. This further leads to the closure of memory bank. You get frustrated and leave the examination room. When the mental pressure eases and brain waves fall down to normal beta range, suddenly the answers you were hunting so desperately a few minutes ago flash suddenly into your mind. You told yourself that you know the material, and sure enough you did but not when you needed to. The mistake you made was "to force yourself to recollect." And this force or mental pressure leads to failure and what you got was the opposite of what you asked or prayed for.

Your failure to get the desired result may be consequence of mentally making and visualiing following of the few statements:

- Things are getting worse.

- I will never get an answer.

- I see no way out

- It is hopeless.

- I don't know what to do.

- I am all mixed up. And so on.

When you use such statements, you get no response or cooperation from your hidden impressions of memory bank. Imagine that you got into a taxi and instructed the driver with a half dozen different directions. He would become hopelessly confused. He might refuse to take you anywhere. Even if he tried to follow your instructions, chances are that he would not be able to. Where you would end up is anybody's guess.

V. HOW TO GET YOUR DREAMS REALISED

The act of visualising opposition creates opposition. If your attention is focused on the obstacles in obtaining what you desire, it is no longer concentrating on the means to obtain your desire. In this process, impressions of obstacles obstruct your desire not getting realised. Therefore, there must be harmonious union or agreement between the two faculties (Conscious mind and Intellect) of our objective mind to unlock and activate the powerful impression of subjective mind and to realise our dreams and prayers.

When there is no longer any quarrel between the different parts of our objective mind (Conscious mind and Intellect), our prayer will be answered. If you visualise the reality of the fulfilled desire and feel the thrill of accomplishment and where opposition is completely absent, your hidden impressions brings about the realisation of your desire.

Many great people solved all this dilemmas and problems by the play of their controlled, directed and disciplined visualisation by their third eye. They never visualised any opposition in their prayers but only affirmation in their prayer. They know whatever they visualise and feel sure that it will and must come to pass.

Affirmative prayers mobilise all the mental and spiritual law of our subconscious mind. Their law is true for good ideas, but it holds true for bad ideas as well. Consequently, if you use your hidden impressions negatively, it brings trouble, failure and confusion. When used constructively, it brings guidance, freedom and peace of mind.

10

MEMORY SYSTEM

Now let us see the last system of being, "The Memory System". (Its faculties are Subconscious mind and Unconscious mind, which can be called memory bank). **Impressions of every action, observation and imagination in Subconscious Mind and un-conscious mind are called Memory.**

The memory bank or The Treasures of Impressions are known as "Sanskar". The Psychoanalysts say that it is the sleeping mind or involuntary mind or even female mind. (Because female controls the male now-a-days, similarly female mind controls the male mind that is conscious mind).

WHAT IS A MEMORY BANK?
It is our inner garden: This storehouse is also known as a garden. Soul is the gardener. As the soul plants the seeds of thoughts with the help of an implement known as intellect, in the garden of Subconscious mind, so shall it reap in the body of environment. Imagine your subconscious mind as a bed of rich soil that will help all kinds of seeds to sprout and flourish, whether good or bad. If you sow thorns, you will reap thorny plants and if you sow roses, there will flourish a rose garden in the body of environment. Every thought is cause and every condition is an effect. This is the reason it is so essential that you take charge of your thoughts through enhanced power of third eye.

Begin now to sow thoughts of peace, happiness, right action, good will and prosperity. Think quietly and with conviction on these qualities. Continue to plant these wonderful seeds of thought in the garden of your subconscious mind and you will reap a glorious harvest. Once you begin to control your thought processes with the help of your intellect, you can apply the powers, which are hidden in your storehouse to solve any problem or difficulty.

If you repeatedly say to your memory bank, "I cannot do it," your memory will create the same environment in the body and mind and you will feel incapable of doing it.

It is like Software of Human Computer: Let us understand this with one more example. Your body is like a ship. You are the navigator of the ship. You navigate this ship with the computerised cabin devices. This cabin can be compared to the brain of the body. The software in these computerised devices is known as memory data. As you press the required button, so is the response from these devices, which create conditions for smooth navigation. Similarly, your memory bank receives order from you through conscious mind and intellect and it responsed accordingly through physical body for navigating life in the ocean of the world. Be sure, your subconscious mind follows only your orders. If you press the button of fear, worry and anxiety through the thought system of your conscious mind and visualise the same things through your third eye (The Intellect), your subconscious mind or memory banks will act accordingly and will activate fear syndrome in the physical body and the same will be reflected through the face which is also known as the index of the mind.

It is the Basis of Our Consciousness: Subconscious mind or Impressions (sanskar) is a major manifestation of human consciousness (soul). It can be compared to a receptacle that contains habits, tendencies, personality traits, memories, values, beliefs, learning, talents, instincts etc. The quality of activities of the other two manifestations of human soul i.e. mind and intellect are based on the quality of sanskar because it is the "sansar" (World) of our inner lives. It gives the soul its specific configuration, just as each compound has a specific chemical configuration, depending on which it reacts.

It is the Archives of All Previously Recorded Experiences: It is the store of the complete data of the soul's roles in the entire life on this world stage and this is the basis of our individual uniqueness. Impressions (Sanskar), being the receptacle of original attributes, virtues, values and all the experiences, project thoughts, desires or feelings on the mind's screen initiating either positive or negative chain of awareness, thought, decision, action and experience depending on the state of soul consciousness or body consciousness respectively. A thought, desire or feeling arises in human mind based on past experiences recorded in memory bank.

It Influences Our Personality: There have been innumerable small and big events in the past, which have exerted their influences on our personality and have moulded our characters but which we do not often recognise consciously. Their influences lie in overt or dormant forms. These have become a part of our lives. Our present attitudes, beliefs, fears, prejudices and all that gives us a pattern of unconscious or subconscious behaviour have been formed of these events. The negative experiences of the recent past get projected as negative thoughts, desires or feelings frequently because they are at the top of the stockpile of experiences in the receptacle of sanskar. Even our obsessions, our temper, our lifestyle is because of these. Some of these memories can perhaps be retrieved under special conditions or with the help of hypnotism or drugs. These implicit or latent memories determine, in part what we do and these influence us all the time.

It is this kind of memory to which Freud and psychiatrists of his school of thought give a very great significance. Comparing it to a glacier, which has 5/7th of its mass under water, these unconscious memories form a major part of one's personality and a forceful factor that influence its behaviour. These bear heavily on self. All brain-scientists, psychologists and psychiatrists agree that it is this, which gives continuity to one's personality. It is this unconscious memory, which gives a unified character or personality in man's normal state of wakefulness from moment to moment.

In Sanskrit language, these dispositions or unconscious memories, which are the result of previous actions, are called **impressions (sanskars)**. It is these, which give unity to the self. The self coordinates the information received from various senses into various parts of the brain and gives to it an experimental unity without which the encoded memory would be meaningless.

Thus, when the conscious personality has its memories at subliminal or infraliminal level, it can be designated as "subconscious" or "unconscious mind".

It is the Seat of Long Term and Permanent Memory: Subconscious mind has the power to do anything on the basis of permanent information stored in it. It is the power of the subconscious mind that makes our heart to beat about 72 times per minute regularly for 60 to100 years. At any time, the subconscious is aware of many body functions including blood pressure, heartbeats, body temperature, chemical balances, blood flow, digestion, assimilation, taking care of emergencies etc

It is well known to psychologists that we can consciously be aware of only 7+2 or 7-2 items at a time. But our subconscious mind can be aware of a large number of items at a time for a longer period.

It is Not Under Our Conscious Control But Intellect Can Control it by The Power of Visualisation: The subconscious mind keeps controlling the function of heart, digestion, circulation, breathing etc. through eternally impressed processes, which are independent of conscious control. It accepts what is impressed upon it or what you consciously create by way of impression of new beliefs and ideas with the help of third eye. Subconscious mind does not reason things out as our intellect does. Intellect has the power to discriminate, judge and visualise a new idea, to make an impression in subconscious mind to form a belief, but subconscious mind acts only according to what is fed in it. Our subconscious mind is like a bed of soil that accepts any kind of seeds good or bad. Our thoughts are seeds. Sub- conscious mind never engages in proving whether these thoughts are good or bad, true or false. It only responds according to the nature of our thoughts and suggestions impressed through third eye.

The power of visualisation is the basis of **mind programming**. Mind programming means that if we can put information in a person's subconscious mind through his third eye, we can modify the person's behaviour. Conscious mind alone cannot put the information without the help of intellect in subconscious mind.

Self-Awareness and Practice of Rajyoga can Dig Out Virtues from Our Memory Bank: Through the practice of soul consciousness and Rajyoga we will be able to dig out the original attributes of the soul from the bottom of the stockpile in the receptacle of sanskar. Thus, the positive chain of awareness -thought-decision –action and experience get repeated every time we practise Rajyoga. With continued practice of Rajyoga, the receptacle of sanskar gets filled with positive experience of the original attributes, virtues and values. **With this change in the self, the world changes.**

The Subconscious Mind can be Programmed Through Hypnotic Suggestions: A skilled hypnotist may suggest to one of his students in the hypnotic state that her back itches, to another that his nose is bleeding, to another that she is a marble statue, to another that she is freezing and the temperature is below zero. Each one will follow out the line of his particular suggestion totally oblivious to all those surroundings that do not pertain to the hypnotic suggestion.

11

MENU OF SUBCONSCIOUS MIND OR TYPES OF IMPRESSIONS

TREASURES IN THE STOREHOUSE OF MEMORY BANK
Following types of impressions are there in the Records of our Memory bank or Subconscious mind.

1. IMPRESSIONS OF STANDARD FUNCTIONING SYSTEM (STANDARD FILES OF MEMORY BANK WHICH HAS THE RECORDS OF POSITIVE, PURE, ELEVATED AND POWERFUL THOUGHTS)

- Regulation of heartbeat, blood circulation, pulse rate, respiration, maintaining body temperature, standard secretion of hormones & enzymes, maintaining normal biochemistry of blood, digestion, assimilation (transmitting food into tissue, blood muscles, bones etc.) and controlling of all vital functions.

  It starts working automatically from Autonomous nervous system functioning (involuntary actions) from the day the soul enters into a human body. No one teaches it. It is inbuilt mechanism within the memory of soul, which functions without remote control and round the clock whether we are awake or sleep.

- All basic qualities (primary virtues) of a soul or spirit that is of knowledge, peace, purity, love, joy, bliss and power and secondary virtues such as harmony, honesty, maturity, politeness etc.

- Vast source of our ideals, aspirations and altruistic urges.

- Solutions of all problems, vast information about creativity, art, science and everything. It has infinite intelligence and boundless wisdom.
- It has secrets of universe and infinite potential, which can do miracle.

- It is also known as **sixth sense or intuitive mind.**

- All spiritual powers, higher consciousness and supra consciousness.

2. IMPRESSIONS OF NECESSARY INFORMATION

- Information related to daily routine work, or day-to-day activities.

- Professional knowledge, skills and general informations of day-to-day affairs.

- Images of many persons and personality with whom we interact.

- Present identity, knowledge of music of own choice, various arts, cultures and customs etc.

- Vivid scenes of past happy moments and future realistic plans.

- Day to day information acquired by self-study, and through electronic & print media.

- Sad moments of Past incidents or accidents, Future fantasies, Future apprehensions, anxieties and fears (false evidences appearing real).

3. IMPRESSIONS OF WASTE INFORMATION

- Vivid scenes of past sad moments and accidents.

- Images of future unrealistic plan and fantasies or unrealistic daydreams.

- Impressions of vicious acts like lust, greed, anger, ego, attachment etc.

- Unrealistic images which lead to apprehensions, worry, anxiety, fears, depression etc.

- Under confidence and inferiority complex and low Syndrome (laziness, procrastination, frustration and pessimistic approach of life).

- Irritative tendencies

4. IMPRESSIONS OF NEGATIVE INFORMATION

- Images of habitual offences and vicious scenes impressed upon memory either due to continuos visualisation of imaginary vicious acts, by reading pornographic materials or continuous watching sinful acts in movies or TV serials or video CD, MMS clips etc.

- Images of porn pictures, which creates intense negative emotions for vicious acts and violence.

- Impressions of negative behaviour, reactive tendencies, humiliating incidents, or revengeful ideas etc., which fuel negative emotions to commit crime.

- Images of ego, lust, greed, jealousy hatred etc.

- Impressions of negative propaganda or suggestions by family, friends, public or media, which cause distress and depression.

Subconscious and Unconscious Mind are like VCD/DVD player, Conscious mind is like screen and Intellect is the eye

Conscious mind is the screen of human beings computer. Subconscious mind is the VCD or DVD player which automatically keeps playing various VCD/DVD, sending many images of various fields on to the screen of conscious mind and through intellect (the third eye). Soul keeps on viewing these images and data, selects it, discriminates it, judges it and orders the motor organs of the body to execute the decisions and feels accordingly.

Thus whatever thoughts, beliefs, opinions, theories or claims we write, engrave or impress on our subconscious mind, we will experience them as the objective manifestations of circumstances, conditions and events. What we write on the inside, we will feel or experience on the outside. Thus we have two sides of our life – objective and subjective, visible and invisible, thoughts and its manifestations.

If you click on negative menu of subconscious mind and think negatively, destructively, and viciously, these thoughts generate destructive emotions and these negative emotions interfere with standard function of involuntary system and thus cause diseases in the body like heart trouble, hypertension, anxieties etc. And again these worries, anxieties, fear, and depression interfere with the normal functioning of the heart, lungs, stomach and intestines. Thus it becomes a vicious circle because these negative patterns of thoughts keep interfering with the harmonious functioning of standard system of our subconscious mind. The law of action and reaction is universal. Our thoughts are the actions and reactions are the automatic response of our subconscious mind to our thoughts.

Therefore, keep your objective mind busy with the expectations of the best, and your subconscious minds will faithfully reproduce your habitual thinking. Visualise the happy ending or solutions to your problems and feel the thrill of accomplishment.

12

WORKING LAWS OF MEMORY BANK

Our memory bank is automatically governed by a set of laws. We must know that laws make changes in our lives style. These laws are as follows:

1. Law of Belief: The belief of our mind is the strong impressions of thoughts visualised by the third eye or seen by the two eyes of physical body and experienced it to be true. Belief does not mean faith in same ritual, ceremony, form, and institution or formula, it is talking about belief itself – simply thought of our mind.

All our experiences, events, conditions and acts, which are reproduced by our memory bank, are the reactions to our thoughts, with which we trigger it. A firm belief activates the hidden potential of memory bank to bring about the result. A thought is an input in our conscious mind, which acts as memory trigger, or incipient action and the reaction is the response from our memory bank that corresponds to the nature of our thoughts, which entered into our memory bank.

Thus our memory bank acts like an ATM machine. As you press the button so is the response from the machine. **Fill your bank (ATM Machine) with the concept of harmony, health, peace, goodwill, eternal varities and truths of life and wonders will happen in your life and you will move onward, upward and Godward.**

You will get what your memory bank is filled with. Stop filling your memory bank with the false belief, wrong opinions, superstitions and fears, which has plagued our human kind.

2. Law of Self-Preservation: Impressions of natural instincts preserve our physical body by constant renewal processes. In almost eleven month our whole physical body is changed. Our stomach lining is replaced every five days. Our skin gets replaced once a month, our skeleton in every three months, even the DNA which holds the genetic material holding memories of millions of years of evolutionary time, the actual raw material of DNA, the carbon, the hydrogen, the nitrogen – comes and goes every six weeks like migratory bird. Our physical body of two years ago is dead and gone and this is the clinching proof of soul's self-preservation and also a proof of a "LIFE AFTER DEATH"

We are riding these molecules of body but we are not the molecules we ride. This skin comes and goes every month. It reincarnates once a month, but it does not forget to give the feeling of pleasure and pain. Our stomach cells change every five days, but they do not forget how to make hydrochloric acid as they incarnate and reincarnate every five days. With the above example it is quite obvious that we are not our physical bodies but we are riding our physical bodies with inbuilt impressions of self- preservation instincts in our memory bank or subconscious mind which keep functioning automatically without the knowledge of our conscious mind and intellect.

The Greek philosopher Herculite has rightly said that you should think of the human body as something like a river. Just like you cannot step into the same river twice because the new water is flowing in, similarly the real you (Soul) cannot step into the same flesh and bones twice.

This is proved scientifically. When we breathe in and out we breathe in 1022 atoms from every where else and every time we breathe out 1022 atoms. And these atoms have their origin in every cells of our body. So at the atomic level we are sharing our organs with each other.

3. Law of Substitution: According to the law of substitution, you can activate the impressions of the joy of freedom by your third eye, which can recondition your memory bank. If you have activated the impressions of negative thoughts and conditioned your memory bank negatively, you could also activate the impressions of positive thoughts and recondition your memory positively by the law of substitution of your memory bank.

If your third eye took you to wrong habits and stressed life, it now can take you to freedom and peace of mind too. By the law of substitution, you visualise the images of freedom, sobriety and perfection and feel the thrill of accomplishment. When fear knocks the door of the mind, let faith in God and all good things substitute the fear. **By the law of substitution only, you can get rid of bad habits and negative thought patterns.**

4. Law of Concentrated Attention or Visualisation: According to this law the idea or any scene that realises itself is the one to which we give the most concentrated attention or visualise vividly. Due to concentration or more attention on thoughts or ideas by our objective mind, the related impressions of memories get quickly activated and realised in practical life. These are the powerful thoughts or ideas, which are enveloped with the power of emotion to get quickly visualised and realised by our subconscious mind. When you are most attentive, to the idea of failure, it is failure that the subconscious mind brings into reality. The fear of failure itself creates the experience of failure by the law of concentration.

If you concentrate on confidence, courage and power, your memory bank will reflect the same. Whatever be your mental picture of attention or concentration, your subconscious mind will bring it to happen as per the law of concentration.

5. Law of Compulsion: Repeating the thoughts or repeating the acts over a period of time from active impressions in memory bank. After that it becomes a second nature apart from our natural nature (first nature), which becomes a habit. Later on the human being gets placed under the compulsion of a habit.

This is known as the law of compulsion. If you repeat a negative thought and keep drinking or smoking or doing any bad habits regularly over a period of time, you will place yourself under the compulsion of these negative thoughts and habits. You will have the temptation of doing it automatically according to the law of compulsion. That is why people feel incapable of giving up their bad habits or negative thoughts and emotions, which are hunting their mind with fear, worry and anxiety.

The active impressions of bad habits and negative thoughts start interfering the state of mind under the law of compulsion despite our mental effort or mental coercion against the bad habits. This leads further to frustration, depression and mental paranoia. Law of compulsion of our memory bank makes our destructive habit to operate automatically like involuntarily action.

6. Law of Observation: If we observe any event or scene with involvement of all sense organs, it gets registered as it is seen. That is why we remember our childhood so vividly. In childhood, there are no negative or waste thoughts, therefore the impressions of childhood remains forever and a child is called the father of the man. With the power of observations we can register anything in our memory for longer duration.

7. Law of Memory Languages: As our computer has got programming languages, similarly our human computer has also got unique languages for mind programming. Only these languages get registered in our memory bank. If we want to improve our memory power, we must communicate with our memory bank in these languages only.

FOLLOWING FOUR TYPES OF LANGUAGE PROGRAMME OUR MINDS:

1.Image: Image of any things automatically impressed in our memory. That is why we recollect the faces of any previously seen person but unable to recollect the name of him.

2. Music: Music too gets impressed automatically in our memory, but lyrics do not get impressed. That is why we feel more relaxed when we listen the music or do humming with music. Alpha music relaxes all muscle and cells of the body.

3. Colour: Colour is also the language of mind. That is why colourful things attract our attention and register the impressions of the things in memory. Visualisation of colours not only tunes our inner body (energy body) but also removes the body pains, backache and muscle pain. For that reason only, infrared rays (Heat therapy) are given during Physiotherapy exercise to remove the muscle pain. Visualisation of "Red" Colour and pinpointing the energy of Red Colour to the Pain affected region gives more relaxation and relief.

4. Art: Art is the creativity of mind, which easily gets impressed in memory. That is why any movie, TV serials or any advertisement (Creative Arts) creates lasting impressions in our memory. **Rajyoga meditation is a mental art used for reconditioning and de-conditioning of our memory.**

13

MINDFULNESS:
ANCIENT SYSTEM OF MEMORY

Our contemporary science defines many different types of memory, depending on different types of brain functions, and based on the neuronal connections. **The ancient understanding of memory was less physical and more psycho- spiritual.**

Memory, in the ancient traditions, is not merely located in physical cerebrum but becomes deeply ingrained in the subtle body in the form of *sanskara* (processed conditioning and modulations of the subtle body). It is on the model of the subtle body, as on a mould, that our physical bodies are then formed, deformed and reformed.

The Sanskrit word for memory is *Smriti* (pronounced in different parts of India as *smriti or smruti,* 'r' here is a vowel). In the Yoga-Sutras of Patanjali, the word occurs in two different meanings: **anubhuta – vishaya – a – sam – pra – moshahsmrtih** (sutra 1.11), **which means an experienced object not being lost from the mind is memory.** This definition is limited so as to explain it as a *Vriti,* or an operation of the mind to be brought under control to attain Samadhi.

In yoga-sutra 1.20, a view parallel to the Buddhist one is enunciated. Samadhi may be attained by following five different methods including *smriti.* **Here smriti is not merely memory but the practice of mind fullness. Mindfulness is very refined form of attention, a state of awareness.**

We need to view these two denotations of smriti as inter linked. When Krishna says: **From anger arises stupefaction (sammoha), from stupefaction the confusion of smriti.** He is talking of the loss of mind fullness. So at the end of the Bhagavad Gita we hear Arjuna exclaim:

"My stupefaction (*moha*) has vanished, mindfulness has returned".

MEMORY AND EMOTIONAL CONFUSIONS

Our memory and emotional states are closely linked. All our confusions are emotional ones. They befog the mind and rob it of its pleasant clarity. Actually concentration is not any effort,it is just clearing the mind of its emotional confusions. Once the fog is lifted, the sun shines clearly. **A clear mind remembers, a confused mind forgets**.

CAUSES OF EMOTIONAL CONFUSION

The prevalence of *"Tamas"*: *"Tamas"* does not indicate stagnancy but stability from the past lives' purification through *Tapasya*. Because of deep inward urge the interest in outward matters is absent and the child appears dull but may excel in spiritual attitudes and in certain arts that can be practised in solitude, and so forth.

Dullness of Intelligence as past karmic effect: For example, a person with much pride in scholarship and intelligence may be born 'stupid'. Intelligence is of many types but memory and intelligence are closely linked.

Lack of Spiritual Preparations on the part of parents: It is to be defined as below:

1. Mother's malnourishment during pregnancy so that the foetus does not receive all the nutrients needed to develop the strength or even the morphology of the neuro cerebral system. So also during lactation.

2. Child's malnourishment so that, again, the nutrients required for developing the cerebral systems are in dearth.

Lack of Training in Education: Lack of training of how to use the mnemonic faculties, associational memory triggers, and of analytical faculties resulting in non-comprehension are the common problems of emotional confusion and loss of memory power.

Overdependency on Technology: The 'mental mathematics' so common up to the time of our grand fathers, is no longer known and without the calculator one cannot cube 25. Everything is noted down in a computer and nothing remembered.

Overfeeding: The energy needed to digest food due to overeating is more. Very less energy is spared for sharpening the mind that keeps becoming dull and less perceptive.

Sleep Deprivation: That is a common phenomenon in the urban industrial countries and communities.

Bad Habits: Alcohol and mind-altering drugs have long-term effects and weaken the memory system.

Stress: Tension and stresses cause lack of relaxation, which reduce concentration power, and weaken the memory system.

Emotional Befogging: This happens even if the neuro cerebral systems are well developed. It is due to waste and negative thoughts occupying the screen of mind and befogging it.

Lack of Interest: Lack of interest in or love for the subject, person, etc. to be remembered is one of the main causes of memory loss.

Information Overload: Nowadays people have become more informative and the loads of general information without any mental filing system have led to more confusion and loss of memory. The general and unwanted information have impaired emotionally and people have become more confused.

Problem of Recall: The problem is not often so much in memorising by mnemonic faculties, as in recalling the things.

Everything we perceive even unconsciously, with any of our senses, is stored in our instruments of consciousness. But when we need any part of these stored data, we cannot get to the right file.

We know that the human mind is capable of enormous feats of memory. Even now there are thousands who memorise entire epics. The number of the Hafiz – who recites the entire Quaran Sharif by heart – in India alone is over 45,000 and those who recite portions of the Veda are at the last count reduced to 20 millions in India. Among those who recite the entire Bhagvad Gita or the *Chandi- patha* daily, approximately 3,000 odd register Sanskrit as their first language. There must be several hundred who memorised all 4,000 sutras of Panini's grammar at a very early age. Even many illiterate mothers and grand mothers of ours sang entire *Kandas* of the Ramayana as we slept in their laps.

But the literate person seems happy with his inability to memorise a single dialogue from Macbeth.

The transfer of the oral form of literature to the written form has been one of the instruments of memory impairment.

METHODS TO IMPROVE MEMORY POWER:

Clearing Emotional Befogging: One looks deep within to see that emotions like anger, fear, remorse, self-doubt. uncertainty, jealousy and insecurity are befogging the mind. One must learn to clear the mind by methods like *Chitta prasanana,* making the mind clear and pleasant through *maitri (*universal friendliness)*, karuna (*compassion)*, mudita (*love*) and upeksha* (indifference) (yoga sutras of patanjali 1.33) or the practice of *manasa-tapas (*mental asceticism).

The mental ascetic practice consists of making the mind clear and pleasant, a moonlike innocent and pure in quality, nature of a meditative and contemplative stage, filled with silence, control over oneself, purification of emotions and sentiments. (Bhagvad gita 17.16).

Practicing Certain Yoga-Asanas and Pranayamas: It is advised to practice 'The Shirsasana' (inverted ones) that supply extra blood flow towards the brain. The headstand is the supreme one of these but it is not for everyone. Pranayamas, not all, but the ones appropriate for memory improvement like Bhramari Pranayama, Udgiata pranayama (chanting of 'OM' for detoxifying the mind and brain) and Anulome-Vilome Pranayam. Shavasana (relaxation practices) is very good for complete relaxation of body and mind.

Practicing concentration exercises: These need to be learnt from a yoga master. *You can learn in detail at any Rajyoga Education Centre of Brahmakumaris in your localities. In my view Rajyoga techniques for concentration is the best one.*

Train your Mind with Mnemonic Faculties: There are many wellknown mnemonic methods for the improvement of memory such as creating mental associations with words or forms. However, these methods help only trigger the memory of the 'little' factors and do not much contribute to the general improvement of the mind –brain relationship. **A few chapters are there in this book to train you with mnemonic systems and memory triggers.**

MNEMONIC EXERCISES (USED BY *VEDA-PATHINS*)

There are many complex mental exercise for improving the attention span and memory. There are a number of other methods using words (specially the Vedic ones).
There are primarily eight verbal permutations in the traditions: *jataa, maalaa, shikhaa, rekhaa, dhavaja, danda, ghana and ratha.* These may be learnt from the Veda- *pathins. These mnemonic devices have been used for the thousands of years that the Vedas have been memorised by heart.*

Diets for Brain Nourishment: These are suitable for a mother to take in preparation for a pregnancy and during pregnancy to help form a child's brain, during lactation, to nourish the same, and after that for the child. For example:

1. Judicious use of almonds and saffron in milk. It is advisable to take saffron at night, almonds in morning prepared in the traditional Indian way.

2. Certain applications of ghee, in defined quantities can be taken. Some of the Ayurvedic herbs can be ingested or massaged into the head. Certain Ayurvedic herbs such as brahmi, jyotishjmati etc. are good for brain nourishment. A qualified Ayurvedic physician can prescribe the correct doses and frequency.

Practice Mindfulness: The Key of Memory: Mindfulness is the total philosophical concept of the equation of memory and practice. The verb root *smriti* means both remembering and practicing mindfulness. Without mindfulness there can be no remembering. One can go into this equation in great detail but here we must restrain ourselves.

Phonetically the verb, *mana* (from which are derived the words *Manu, manushya, mantra, manas,* Hindi *mana* for mind, *manana, muni, Mauna, menos*) is related also to the verb for practicing to memorise. The Paninian verb root *mna* (pronounced *mnaa*) cognate to the words like 'mnemonic', 'something related to memory'.

Zeus and the Goddess era had a temporary liaison from which was born Mnemosyne (or Mnamosyna), the titanic Goddess of memory. It is she who is the inventor of words, in the Greek mythology, and the mother of nine muses (nine aspects of Saraswati, one might say). She is the memory or remembrance (mneme) herself.

For memory and remembrance, mind (manas) is the instrument and mantra is an invariable aid. The tradition has it that when a text is revealed to a sage or rishi, he recited to the disciples by practice. (They sit facing him which is the literal meaning of ' *abhi* + *asa*= *abhyasa'* and practice to memorise the same). Then they go off on their own to sit under a tree or by river, or by the sacred fire of *homa*, facing the river or the fire *(abhi +asa)* and recite to memorise. This process is known as *Svadhyaya* (studying on one's own).

But in the yogasutras the word 'mantra' is used for mental recitation in meditation because, as the text is recited, slowly it is assimilated into the mind. At which point the practice becomes *japa*.

Thus **listening, mentating, contemplating, reciting, memorising, doing *japa* for concentration, purifying and clearing the mind** are all different shades of the same spectrum. Memorising without contemplating will be futile.

Thus it was that preservation of texts, improvement of memory and practice of contemplation and japa, as well as all **the practices of mindfulness, altogether formed what we may now term as smriti – yoga.**

Practise Yoga-Nindra: This is one direction of interiorisation. There is another, which is called yoga-nindra (yogic sleep or conscious rest), converting sleep state into a step towards *Samadh*i. However, true yoga-nindra is not easy to come by. It may be defined in several stages as follow:

1. Being aware of one's sleep state and directing it.

2. While producing delta brain waves that indicate non-REM deep sleep, one should remain aware of one's surroundings.

3. One's meditation and sleep are simultaneous- while the surface mind sleeps, the deeper mind meditates.

4. Entry into the heart cave, permitting neither mantra nor thought. This state may come during the various breath preparations that are taught to train the mind to enter yoga-nindra.

During yoga-nindra, one may learn a language or another subject, do quick memory work, remember forgotten facts, become a master of sleep, needing no more than two sleep cycles (three to four hours of sleep every 24 hours), may heal certain ailments and alleviate acute pains in oneself, may write a new constitution or compose an epic, may receive intuitive knowledge such as a new scientific theory or a mantra.

The depth in yoga nindra depends on how well one has been prepared, how deep the teachers own experience is, how emotionally balanced and self-controlled the practitioner is.

Manage Your Time: Two of the most precious segments of our 24-hour day that we waste are:

a. While we are falling asleep, the time is wasted in unnecessary reverie and fantasy.

b. And while we are waking up, the time is wasted in tossing and turning.

These are our most creative times. If one understands the processes of consciousness in these two segments of time, one can create immortal works. While one is falling asleep, ones mind is free of all exterior distractions, but one has not yet entered the sleep state. This twilight period is akin to yoga-nindra. One does need to learn how to use this time.

Purify your Emotions by Interior Resolve (Sankalpa): Just the knowledge of Sanskrit and yoga-nindra as a mere technique will not do it. To clear the mind and to keep unwrinkled, the conquest of anger is the first step in emotional purification. All this accomplishments may take times. Human mind is a creature of habit. Whatever is habitual to us we consider it to be natural. All one needs to do is trigger it, activate it. Any habit can be changed. The mind can be retrained and restrained.

In the theory of neuroplasticity, it is now known that even the functions of the different parts of the brain can be altered and retrained. It can be done through *abhyasa* (Practice).

Sit down, face your goal, and practice. Whatever the mind is taught to do repeatedly, through a quiet interior resolve (sankalpa), that will become mind's habit (the discovery of another hitherto concealed treasure in the nature of mind).

The Deep "Sankalpa" (Power of Intent) is inherent in the very consciousness (chit–shakti) that gives a slight nudge to the layer of mind that is just next underneath the common chattering mind. It is told to take a certain direction to channel thoughts of a particular stream into consciousness. Thus, one may create whatever one wishes.

Recognise your Conscience (Inner Voice of the Soul): Conscience is still, small and peaceful voice within. It is the moral law within. It is the automatic call of the soul based on standard impressions in our memory bank.

Conscience is the light of the soul that burns within the chambers of our psychological heart (subconscious mind). It protests whenever anything unrighteous is done or thought of.

It is also a ledger where our offences are recorded. Conscience threatens, promises, rewards and punishes, keeping all under its control. If conscience stings once, it is an admonition, and twice, it is condemnation.

If anything happens wrong, our conscience immediately responds with its right judgments, which are permanently imprinted in the standard file of our memory bank. It teaches that the ends and means are inseparable. As Gandhiji had said – " through the unprincipled unworthy means, the ends will turn to dust" as is expressed in his following observation:

"Wealth without work, pleasure without conscience, knowledge without character, commerce without morality, science without humanity, worship without sacrifice, and politics without principles."

Conscience always asks, "is it right?" Majority of us have become deaf to its voice, insensitive to its pricks and impervious to its criticism because our routine files of memory have been corrupted due to prevalent rampant corruption.

Once you engage in wrong actions and sinful deeds, you will not hesitate to carry out serious crimes. If you allow one sin to enter and dwell in your conscience, you have the way for the entry of a thousand sins. Your conscience will become blunt and lose its sensitivity. Doing evil deeds will become part of your nature.

A virtuous man alone can hear the soul's inner voice clearly. In a wicked man, this faculty is dead. The sensitive nature of his conscience has been destroyed by corruption. Hence, he is unable to discriminate right from wrong. This applies also to organisations, business enterprises, institutions and governments.

Therefore it is wise to have a clean conscience, recognize it and enjoy freedom from anxieties and worries.

14

BRAIN, MEMORY AND SOUL

Memory is an essential pre-requisite of all learning. It gives continuity and unity of personality. If mind had no memory it would behave as a different person every moment, for it would be cut off from even its immediate past. But we all know from our experience and observation that mind continuously behaves as a unified person, which is aware of its past and has hopes and expectations for the future. So it is an important question whether the mind, which learns and has the faculties of retention, attention and memory, and also has a continuity and unity of self, is not different from the brain or it is a metaphysical entity, apart from the body and the brain.

Neurobiologists and psychologists generally classify memory under three heads: **Short term memory, Long-term memory and Subconscious memory (unconscious memory or implicit memory).** We will briefly discuss all these three.

SHORT-TERM MEMORY

Memory, which lasts for a few seconds or a few minutes, is called 'short term memory'. For example, after searching a telephone number from the telephone directory, we generally hold that number into our memory only for a short while because that number will not be of frequent use to us in future.

Neurologists say that this kind of memory is affected by the neural events, continuing during the rehearsal, so to say of the telephone number. In the present case for example, neuronal activity continues as a circuit so as to keep that telephone number into our attention all the while between the time of looking into the directory and the time of dialing. Similarly circuits of neural activity in the brain continue to hold for us, for a short while, names or facial pictures of some persons, which we would forget soon afterwards.

Obviously, memory according to this explanation is brain based. There can be no denial of the fact that neuronal activity takes place during the processes of learning or memory storage. But there are also other sides to this phenomenon, which are generally overlooked.

For example, a deep reflection would bring this fact into focus of our attention that after all, it is the mind which intends to hold that bit of information for a short while only and therefore it activates the neuronal mechanism of the brain for only that much duration and not longer, and then learning that number there, it attends to another thing or another piece of work. In other words it is the mind which held in memory that telephone number with the help of the neuronal machinery as one holds the directory with the help of one's hand in front of one's eyes and it held it in memory only for the time it needed the number. Therefore as hands are one's instruments of action, so are brain cells or neurons, which the mind employs.

Thus mind is self conscious, it feels, though in a subtle manner that it is using the brain, which either has good ability of retention or has amnesia or has lost this faculty totally because of some injury, trauma, disease, aging or surgical removal of certain parts. **This self-conscious mind, which either appreciates the faculties of the brain or regrets the loss, is called Soul.**

LONG TERM MEMORY

Memory that endures for days and years is called the Long Term Memory. There are many theories in vogue regarding this kind of memory, the chief among these being, 'The electrophysiological' or 'The synaptic theory' or 'The growth theory of learning'.

There is another theory of long-term memory, which says that memories are encoded in specific macromolecules, in particular in RNA in the brain. But this theory has failed for various reasons. There is yet another theory known as 'chemical theory', which says that bits of information can be transferred from animal to animal by way of injecting certain chemicals which are related to transmitting substances.

But the generally accepted theory now is **the synaptic theory** or the **growth theory of learning**. According to many brain scientists, long-term memories are somehow encoded in the neuronal connectivity of the brain. When the process of learning or memory storage takes place, micro growth of synaptic connectivity of nerve cells in the brain also takes place. What happens is that, as a result of sensory stimulus, the information in the form of electrical waves goes to the brain through the sensory pathways where it results in synaptic activation of neurons. This leads first to the synthesis of RNA manufactures in the brain, by a special kind of metabolism, proteins and other macromolecules, which are required for the micro-growth of the synapses connectivities of the nerve cells and for increase in membrane and chemical transmission. Thus the existing synaptic connectivities become hyperactive and more efficient, or there is micro growth of new synapses. Memory is encoded in these synaptic connectivities. There are, in this way, structural and functional changes and it is estimated that the synaptic micro growth and the process of encoding of memory takes from 30 minutes to 3 hours. This information coded in the synaptic formation, serves as the data bank of memory.

Physiological experiments have also indicated that the modifiable synapses, which could be responsible for memory, are excitatory and are there in great majority in the cerebral cortex and the hippocampus (the granule cells of the hippocampus and the purkyne cells of the cerebellum). These are concerned with learning. There is also evidence that these synapses regress during disuse.

THE SUBCONSCIOUS OR IMPLICIT MEMORY

We have already considered the short term and long-term memory. Let us now consider the subconscious, unconscious or the implicit memory. This too will prove that the self is different from the brain. What are subconscious or unconscious memories?

There have been innumerable small and big events in the past which have exerted their influence on our personality and have moulded our character but which we do not often recognise consciously. Their influences lie in overt or dormant form. These have become a part of our life. Our present attitudes, beliefs, fears, prejudices and all that gives us a pattern of unconscious or subconscious behaviours, have been formed of these. Some of these memories can perhaps be retrieved under special conditions or with the help of hypnotism or drugs. These implicit or latent memories determine, in part, what we do, and these influence us all the time

The self is that coordinates the information received from various senses into various parts of the brain and gives to it an experiential unity without which the encoded memory would be meaningless. Decidedly therefore reflection on various kinds of memory proves the existence of soul, which uses the mechanism of the brain.

IS THE SOUL ENGAGED IN MEMORY PROCESS?

Now the main question before us is: in the light of the above mentioned evidence from neuro-biology and neuro-surgery which explains how synaptic connectivities work as data banks and which parts of the brain are used for memory storage, what evidence there is that leads us to believe in the existence of a metaphysical entity, called soul or self-conscious mind.

An answer to this can be found by thinking over the process of memory-retrieval. If we do some introspection on how we recall, on demand, the name of a man or some fact stored in our databanks we will be able to discover the truth.

MEMORY RETRIEVAL

It will be observed that whenever we want some information from the databank, we begin to search, so to say, we make a search for synonym, for an appropriate word that can express our ideas in a better way or the name or telephone number of a person who met us a number of years ago. The self or the mind does some sort of probing into the brain so as to retrieve, from these something, which it desires. It requires the brain to deliver the memory to it. During this process of racking our brain and succeeding or failing to get the good delivered, we always experience a very strong dualism involved. **We observe that the self or the mind is separate from the brain, which is like a library, a storehouse or a computer, from which we are trying to have some stored information.**

It will be noticed that when the mind is searching to recover memories, for example, of words, proverbs, ideas, events, pictures, tunes and melodies etc. it is actively scanning through the memory store house. Sometimes it may be easy and sometimes may be difficult to recall the desired bit of information to our memory. In this attempt the mind plays backward and forward looking for the desired answer. Not only that, the retrieved information, a word, a telephone number, the name of a man, a figure etc. is critically scrutinised whether it is accurate and suitable or not when it gets a delivery from the databank. It may judge it to be erroneous, there may be a slight error in the name or the proverb, or the synonym may not be suitable. **So the self or the mind makes a renewed effort at retrieval.** It may again judge the retrieved memory as faulty and so it may make yet another attempt or it may decide to abandon the attempt.

This scrutinising of the retrieved memory clearly shows that there are infact two kinds of memory:

(1) The memory stored in the brain in the synaptic connectivities or in the macromolecules and

(2) The recognition memory, which is applied by the self or the mind in its scrutiny of the retrieval from the brain store.

The conscious self which judges and evaluates the correctness and relevance of the data, delivered to it from the stored memory, is because of its recognition memory, superior to the brain, for it acts as the judge, the assessor and the arbiter. It can accept or reject the data from the stored memory and can also modify it or use it or put it back into the storage.x

We can clearly observe both these types of memory at play. We notice this more clearly when, at times we feel that the mind is under a challenge to recall the desired memory. Physiologically speaking, the mind when looking for a bit of information, is trying to discover the appropriate modules or synaptic connectivities, in the brain. **It is thus clear that it is the mind, which gets the delivery whereas it is the brain, where the mind searches for the desired information**

MIND ADOPTS TRICKS (MEMORY TRIGGERS) TO RETRIEVE DATA FROM THE BRAIN

The difference between the two becomes clearer when we observe the mind adopting some strategies or tricks to discover the required information from the stored memory. The mind says to itself "The name of that man was in some way similar to castophene". Then it says to itself only seconds afterwards "yes, yes it is Christopher; now I remember. It would make use of the psychological law of association and other methods, many of which are given in subsequent chapters in this book. **On such an occasion, when it applies these tricks and strategies it becomes obvious that the brain and the self conscious mind are two different entities, the former is like a data bank and the later uses it as it likes.**

THE BRAIN IS AND COMPUTER

Yet there are many psychologists and scholars who are of the opinion that thinking, judging etc. pertain to the brain which works like a computer. They say that the network of the sensory nerve, which are spread through out the body, conveys messages, images or information to the brain, which deciphers these, thinks over a way out and hatches out plans to meet the situation. They say that an electronic wave rises from the brain to bring out a response to the stimulus. They thus assert that there is no mind separate form the brain, which works like a computer.

But in saying this, they forget that a computer is only a special type of machine and machines and instruments are made of material parts, cannot move of themselves and for themselves. The one that sets it moving, that presses the button, fills it with fuel, overhauls it when needed or does many other things related to it and sets it to purpose is an engineer, an operator or a mechanic- a living worker, a conscious person.

MEMORY CANNOT BE EXPLAINED IN THE ABSENCE OF PERMANENT SELF

We all know very well that besides the perceptions, every human being has memory. If there is only a rapid succession of perceptions then who has the memory or the faculty of recollection? Let us explain this question by means of an example.

Suppose that I saw a boy twenty years ago there was a perception of his form and figure. Now, after this long period, during which millions of other perceptions have taken place, I see him again. The boy has grown up to be a man in the meanwhile. There is a perception and he notices the similarities and the changes. If there have only been perceptions and there was no permanent perceiver, then who links up the past and the present perceptions, choosing it out of millions of other perceptions. As a bundle of perceptions each morning get recorded, who was it that recollected a perception that is now twenty years old? Physically, I am not today what I was yesterday or, say twenty years ago. Considered, as a perception also my existence is not what it was twenty years ago. But the knowledge is vouchsafed only to that person who has observed the boy today and also twenty years earlier. **This, therefore, proves that there is a permanent self who perceives and recollects.**

SOME CASES OF HYPNOTIC REGRESSION REVEALS MEMORIES OF PAST LIVES

A case was reported in Sept.1982 issue of the monthly "Mirror" published from Mumbai. Its reporter had interviewed J V

Rao a hypnotist based in Dadar Mumbai. Mr Rao mentioned a curious case of regression. A christian girl of 18 in a hypnotic show in Bombay started speaking Italian. She revealed that in one of her previous lives during the period of Mussolini she had been born as a man in Italy. She narrated how her that life had ended in a road accident. After the hypnotic state was over she could neither utter Italian language nor could she narrate even a single incident, which she had stated while in hypnosis. In her present life she had never gone out of India. She did not have even the slightest notion how Italian language sounds.

Two other clear cases were mentioned in the Sep 1982 issue of the monthly 'Mirror'. One of these related to a well-known American lawyer who professed to be a hard-core atheist. When he was hypnotically regressed he gave out the details of his former life as a prostitute. The other case relates to a high class French lady. In the state of hypnosis she revealed that she had been beheaded in her previous life. She said that she had been detected to be carrying on a clandestine love affair with a Britisher and this becomes the cause of her being murdered. There are several other cases revealed by various hypnotherapists that prove the existence of past memories in the subconscious mind, the faculty of soul.

The famous American hypnotherapist Mr Brian Weiss's books titled 'Many Lives Many Masters', 'Love is only real', 'Messages from masters', and 'The same soul many bodies', have thrown enough light on memory of the soul. It clearly proves that the memory is not the function of the brain but it is the faculty of the soul, which is eternal. It is just like the "SIM" card of a mobile. Our body is like a mobile instrument. As a mobile cannot function without 'SIM', our body cannot function without the soul.

THE SOUL IS NOT ONLY DIFFERENT FROM BRAIN BUT BRAIN PUTS LIMITATIONS ON SOUL

In fact, hypnosis clearly establishes that brain and body put limitations on the expression of consciousness. The cases of exaltation of senses and the mental capacities in the state of hypnosis clearly bring out that the brain and the nervous system are not the causative sources of mental life but are, instead, delimiting factors.

APPARITIONS OF THE DEAD AND CASES OF REBIRTH PROVE THE MEMORY IS THE FACULTY OF SOUL

Mention may also be made of apparitions of the dead. There has been a belief since very early times that those who die prematurely because of some accidents or serious illness or other un-expected causes hover about in the atmosphere in subtle forms for varying periods. Many such stories have been published in books and reputed periodicals from time to time.

The story of previous life, as told by certain children, does not only show that memory is not lost and that events are not totally and forever forgotten but it also shows that memory is retained by man at subliminal or infra liminal level and is an ability of consciousness. It is not a faculty of the brain tissue, for the previous body and brain having been cremated, the person is now able to relate, through the medium of the new brain, which is not yet even fully developed, events of an early life with emotion, feelings and cognition of relationship as in that life. Thus memory is decidedly the faculty of a metaphysical personality, which survives the death and can remember the events of an earlier life.

Evidently such verified cases point to the existence of non-physical self, which survives physical death.

FEELING OF SATISFACTION OR DISAPPOINTMENT PERTAINS TO MIND AND SOUL

Another thing which points to the difference between the mind and the brain is that the mind, after making efforts at recovery or after watching the delivery either feels satisfied or happy or even astonished as one feels when one is able to get a desired piece of information from a book, a file or a diary.

THE ROLE OF BRAIN IN THE FUNCTION OF MEMORY OR MEMORY RETRIEVAL

The brain traces are the impressions left by the events. Those traces are like the coded tunes which are of help to the soul and which facilitate its work. These are like a map to a tourist who has already travelled along the routes delineated in the map or these are like to the notes to a student who is preparing for an examination or they serve as a diary of life events, or a file of proceedings of a meeting. But they are not the person, i.e. the master of the orchestra or a student or a diary keeper or a secretary of the meeting but one who uses proceedings is the conscious person to whom these brain traces or memory tracks or engrams or axions and dendrites serve the purpose of the soul. The existence of the soul is thus a well-established fact.

MEMORY IS THE IMPRESSIONS OF ALL MENTAL AND PHYSICAL ACTIONS OF PAST, PRESENT AND FUTURE IN THE SUBCONSCIOUS OR UNCONSCIOUS LAYERS OF MIND

15

POWERS OF THE THIRD EYE

Visualised experience and a real experience have same effect on our mind. Following are some real examples to understand the experience of power of visualisation.

I. Basketball Training and Visualisation

In a 30 days research experiment on "Basketball training and Visualisation" students were divided into three groups. One group did not practise the game of basketball, the second group practised on playground and the third group practised only in their mind for one-hour daily.

The Results: The group, which did not practise did not improve. The group, which practised improved 24%, and the group, which practised only in mind, improved 23%.

This experiment showed that practising in our mind alone improves sports performance almost as much as doing real practise.

II. PLACEBO AND VISUALISATIONS

It is well known that physicians regularly use placebos, sugar pills or pills with absolutely no real medicinal properties. The patients however are told that the pills are powerful medicine. Countless studies have proved the high effectiveness of those 'mind only' medications.

II.1. In a 1979 study, patients with severely bleeding ulcers were split into two groups. **One** was told that they were taking a new drug that would bring immediate relief.

The second group were told that they were taking on experimental drug, but not much was yet known about its effects. The same drug was administered to both groups.

RESULT: 75% of the first group improved and 25% of the second group improved. The only difference was the patient's expectations through visualisations by their third eye.

II.2. At Harvard University, Dr Beecher researched pain in post-operative patients. Some were administered morphine and some a placebo. The morphine controlled the pain in 52 % of the patients who received it. The placebo controlled the pain in 40% of the patients. **In the other words, the placebo was 75% as effective as the morphine.**

The visualisation expecting the pain relief actually triggered the production of endorphin, the naturally produced opiate chemicals that block the neuro transmitters, which allows the sense of pain to register on the brain.

Many researchers are now convinced that a good proportion of the results from real medication is received from the placebo or halo effect. Since everyone including the doctor knows that extensive testing goes into new drugs, when one is released for use. The doctor expects it to work, the patient expects it to work and it does work.

A placebo works because the third eye finds ways to activate impressions of healing from its memory bank to bring about what you visualise and believe it to happen.

Because of the undoubted power of the third eye to produce healing in patients, doctors worldwide are more and more moving towards holistic medicine. Holistic merely means (w)holistic treating the whole patient, not just his body, but his mind too.

III. THE SUBJECTIVE MIND AND IMAGES

The subconscious mind cannot differentiate between what is real and what we believe is real. It only receives the impressions of images that are visualised by the third eye and acts or reacts with these images in the same ways as it does in real life.

III.1. "Man freezes to death in refrigeration car" the 1964 headline was hardly startling, but the circumstances were:

A man got trapped inside the refrigerator car as the door accidentally slammed on him. When he was found, he had all physical symptoms of having frozen to death. Yet the refrigeration unit was switched off and at no time had the temperature been at or even to freezing. He visualised and his memory system believed that he was going to freeze and his subjective mind had produced the physical effect to create hypothermia and froze him to death.

III.2. IQ tests by Dr. Rosenthal, a California psychologist: Dr. Rosenthal, a California psychologist administered IQ tests to a public school class. He totally ignored the results, but nevertheless divided the class into two groups.

The first group, he informed the teacher, was considerably brighter than the second.

But there was in fact no difference. The children were never told about his conclusion but the teacher was told to treat all the pupils the same.

Eight months later, the grades of the two arbitrarily classified groups were compared. The first group had grades 28% better than the second group and their IQ actually measured higher. Without one word being said, the teacher had managed to communicate, quite subconsciously, a higher expectation of the first group and a lower expectation of the second group, all without the subjects even knowing of it. The teacher had created a better learning environment for the favoured group, and it worked.

IV. VISUALISATION ENHANCES MEMORY POWER

Anything visualised by the third eye gets a place in 'subconscious mind or memory bank. Students can utilise this visualisation technique to memorise their study materials. For example: following 10 words can be memorised by following visualisation exercise easily:

1. Dog 2. Shoes 3. Movie 4. Dragon 5. Cycle 6. Telephone
7. Pen 8. Cold-drink 9. Tiger 10. Tape-recorder

Now visualise a Dog wearing Shoes, going for a Movie in which there is a Dragon riding a Cycle. The cycle hits a Telephone booth. Somebody repairs the damaged phone with the tip of a Pen. The pen is filled with a Cold drink and not with ink. The person serves the cold drink to a Tiger by opening the pen. The tiger begins to dance on a tune played by Tape-recorder.

V. THE THIRD EYE CAN DE-STRESS YOU

The subjective mind and the body are intimately connected. And hence we can use visualisation in a positive way to beat stress and relax.

Keep a mental account of the happier moments of your life you have experienced. Select one of the moments of your happier days by visualising yourself in those moments. Try to feel the pleasant atmosphere and music of appreciation of your happier moment.

"We are not what we think we are but what we visualise we are."

VI. The Third Eye helps to get rid of Diseases

Visualisation by third eye is an effective technique that can be used for treating many stress-related diseases and physical illness such as headaches, muscle spasms, chronic pain and many times even general and situational specific anxiety. For instance, if you are in pain and trying to think of something pleasant, most often it works.

Consciously visualising may take some time to learn. Lots of time is wasted by interruption of another waste and negative images. All you need is some practice. Remember that practice makes you perfect, so try to practise the techniques of visualisation at least thrice a day. With continued practice and determination you can master any technique.

The author of this book has cured his cancer, hepatitis and diabetes by the visualisation power of his third eye besides medication. Remember, medication helps those who help themselves by empowering their third eye.

VII. THE THIRD EYE IS USED FOR HYPNOTHERAPY

Hundreds of women around the world, are experiencing painless childbirth using only hypnotherapy instead of anesthesia. Countless cancer patients swear that hypnotherapy helps to manage the pain of chemotherapy.

Many more use it for effectively eliminating smoking and drugs habits, fears and phobias, depression, anxiety, improving memory and study habits, enhancing sports and stage performance, losing weight, building self esteem, stress management, improving relationship and even exploring the past lives.

WHAT IS HYPNOTHERAPY?

Experts from most healing disciplines agree that the state of a person's subjective mind has direct bearing on behaviour, health and quality of his life.

Hypnotherapy uses techniques of hypnosis to provide direct access to the subjective mind, the most powerful faculty of human being for changing limiting beliefs and experiencing and adding new resources. This allows the mind and body to support and guide new behaviour from the deepest level, thereby creating powerful and lasting changes.

WHAT IS HYPNOSIS?

Hypnosis is a deep state of calm and relaxation. The body is very comfortable and the mind, more alert than the normal state of awareness. **It is a trance state**, characterised by extreme suggestibility, relaxation and heightened visualisation by the third eye. It is unlike sleep as the person is alert throughout. It is often compared to day- dreaming.

In everyday life also people enter hypnosis naturally while watching TV, extensive driving and overwhelmed by nature. We also enter in hypnotic state right before we sleep and upon awakening. It is as if the hypnotism process pops open a control panel inside the brain.

HOW HYPNOTHERAPY WORKS?

With the "access door" to your subjective mind opened by the third eye, the hypnotherapist can re-program your sub-conscious to reverse bad behaviour by connecting an altered response with a good habit. To ease pain and cure illness, hypnotherapy uses the underlying idea that the subjective mind and body are inextricably intertwined when a suggestion is given to the subconscious that the body does not feel pain, or that the body is free of disease, the subconscious actually brings about the changes by activating healing impressions.

The applications of hypnotherapy are growing day by day. Through hypnotherapy we can modify beliefs that no longer serve us and create a new enhanced personality that is confident, secure and functioning in harmony with the mind and universe.

VIII. THE THIRD EYE MAKES IMPOSSIBLE POSSIBLE

The basis of all scientific research and invention is our 'Third eye'. Sub-conscious mind gets opened with intense visualisation by third eye and also provides the clue for scientific research and new inventions. For example:

a. One day James Watt was sitting in front of a stove. A kettle full of water was boiling on the fire. He was looking at it very attentively. James was puzzled on seeing the lid of the kettle move up and down. He wanted an answer to his question. He thought the steam was responsible for the motion of the lid. His constant visualisation in this direction went on to build steam engines that brought a revolution in every sphere of life.

b. Newton saw an apple falling from a tree and constantly visualised why it fell down on the earth instead of going up in the sky? And this led to the invention of theory of Gravitation.

c. Archimedes once taking a bath in a tub shouted, "Eureka, eureka........." and his visualisation moved to unlock his subconscious mind to find the theory of buoyancy which further led to invention of ships and submarines. Then, similarly computers, mobile phones, pilot less aircraft etc are the result of constant and creative visualisation by the soul's third eye.

IX. THE THIRD EYE DEVELOPS A POSITIVE PERSONALITY

Narendranath (the childhood name of Swami Vivekananda) often encountered people of various castes who came to meet his lawyer father. There was a separate room in the house where his father's clients discussed their cases. That room was a place of wonder for Narendranath as it had a number of hookahs of every size and shape. They were kept at a certain distance in every part of the room. Narendranath had once asked his father why there were so many hookahs. His father had said, "People of many castes and ranks come to my office. These hookahs are for people belonging to the various castes and ranks, so that they don't degrade themselves by using the same hookah and lose their caste." Narendranath was puzzled by his father's answer.

So one day he went to the sitting room when nobody was around and started taking a few puffs from each hookah. His father came into the room and was surprised on seeing his son's strange behaviour. He asked Narendranath what he was doing. The boy simply replied, "I am tasting each hookah to see if I lose my caste. But I am the same Narendra." His father was left speechless at this answer.

Such type of spirited visualisation by his third eye moulded the boy Narendra to become world famous personality "Swami Vivekananda." He went on to become the world teacher, who spread the message of brotherhood and equality.

X. THE THIRD EYE DEVELOPS WILL POWER

Visualisation by the third eye develops 'will power' and "turns an idea into a belief". **A belief is an idea that we accept to be true. It can be a fact, a guiding principle, an opinion or a faith in someone or something.** We can have a faith in our teacher or doctor, in the value of being honest or good, in the value of exercise for good health, in our ability to succeed, or in the value of reading newspapers, magazines and books.

A belief can be conscious or subconscious. Conscious beliefs mean that we know that we believe something. Subconscious belief means that we do not even know that we believe something. **Conscious belief is called an idea**, which can be compared to a table top without legs. **The visualisation power of the third eye is a tool, which provides legs to an idea and makes it a sub-conscious belief, which becomes very powerful.** An example of sub-conscious belief is that we accept to be true what we see on the TV, what we hear on the radio and what we read in the newspaper. Thus beliefs are very powerful.

Reflect on following examples:

X.1. Roger Bannister broke the record: In the first half of the 20th century, athletes and trainers believed that human body could not run a mile in four minutes. Then in May 1954, Roger Bannister broke this myth when he ran a 3.59-mile. He constantly visualised by his third eye about victory with such a determination that his subconscious mind activated impressions with a powerful belief (it was just an idea earlier) and gave the signal to his nervous system to achieve physical result to match his visualised image. Following in Banister's stride and believing that they too **could do it**, within one year several others duplicated his feat.

X.2. A soviet weight lifter Vasily Alexeer broke the record: In weight lifting it was believed that 500 pounds was the limit for the human body. Many could lift 499 lbs, but none 500 lbs or more. Then the trainers befooled a soviet weight lifter Vasily

Alexeer about the actual weight of 500.1 pounds but they told him instead that it was only 499 lbs. Vasily Alexeer lifted the weight. Once the belief was broken many other weight lifters were able to lift more than 500 pounds.

XI. THE THIRD EYE PROGRAMMES THE SUBJECTIVE MIND

When enemies attacked and killed the king of Udaipur, Rajasthan, a servant named Panna Dhay saved his son. Finally the boy grew up and became the king. Why do you think he could do it? Was it in the blood (genetics) of the boy? No, he did it because the servant and everybody else told the boy, "You are a prince. You must become the king. The enemy has taken over your kingdom and when you grow up, you must take revenge and defeat the enemy."

Constantly hearing the same message, the child did not go to become a clerk or a businessman but he wanted to become the king. And he was willing to die to achieve his goal. He constantly visualised by his third eye about his features of a future king with his victory over his enemies and thus programmed his subconscious mind, which in turn activated the impressions of courage and valour and made him king.

This historical story shows that people/society can programme our mind if we visualise in positive direction. Unlike the prince, most of us get programmed by wrong messages such as "don't do that...don't take risk...don't be stupid... you are stupid...you are not so good as so and so."

We act not according to what things really are but according to what we expect them to be, believe them to be, visualise them to be. **"Visualisation" said Napoleon, 'rules the world".** He actually rehearsed with his third eye about every battle he ever fought weeks before the event, going over his own tactics, visualising the enemy defences, their reaction and the terrain. Napoleon was 105 years ahead of his time.

When a small baby elephant, is tied with a big strong chain, it tries hard to escape from the chain, but it can not escape. As the elephant grows, the trainers replace the big strong chain by small rope. Surprisingly, the elephant still remains tied to the rope. It probably thinks, "there is no point trying... I know.... I have tried before and failed, I am tied with the rope...............I cannot escape. Thus an elephant mind gets programmed.

How does a negative belief work? A negative or limited belief is like an obstacle. It blocks the impressions of victory and makes our efforts invain.

XII. THE THIRD EYE CREATES CONFIDENCE

Suppose you are asked to speak to a group of 100 people. If you believe you are not good at speaking, you will not be self-confident. As a result, when you stand up and talk you will lack the power, you will assume that you are not speaking well, and you will feel bad. That will have bac effect on your speech. And this will confirm to yourself that you are not good at speaking in public.

The positive beliefs work in the same way. They make positive loops and that maintain the positive beliefs.

XIII. THE THIRD EYE PREPARES THE BODY TO MEET ANY DANGEROUS SITUATION

Suppose a person is walking in the park. He sees something like a snake and imagines in his mind 'it is a snake'. The message of fear is sent to other parts of the brain, then to the spinal cord, and then to the rest of the body. In a very short period, the whole body knows about the danger and prepares itself to face the danger. The heart beat increases, blood pressure increases, breathing become faster. Blood is diverted from the brain to the muscles, the hands and the feet. As a result, the person is ready to fight or to run away. **This well-known phenomenon is called "fight or flight response".** Just the thought 'snake' creates this response. And when he happens to identify the snake like object was not a snake but a rope, this real picture or image changes the whole process and his heart beats and his blood pressure become normal and he laughs at his wrong image of visualisation.

Thus with several above example, it is very –very clear that third eye is very powerful. Visualisation by third eye is not just a thought but it is an obvious and colorful image or we can say that it is a colourful videographs, which resembles the real picture.

Visualisation is actually a form of computation. Visualisation gives calculated and instinctive solutions for future. If Visualisation is dulled, one's computation is seriously handicapped. With daydreaming, for instance, a person can convert a not too pleasant existence into something livable. **Only with Visualisation can one postulate future goals to attain.**

If you take the word Visualisation apart, you will discover that it means merely the postulating of images or the assembly of perceptions into creations, as you desire them. Visualisation is something one does of his free will. Delusion could be said to be something forced upon by his aberrations in images visualised.

XIV. THE POWERFUL THIRD EYE HAS THE HIGHER LEVEL OF "EMOTIONAL QUOTIENT"(EQ)

Emotional Intelligence is the ability of the soul to sense, understand and effectively apply the power and acumen of emotions as a source of human energy, information, trust, creativity and influence. **We can say that it is the ability of a soul to understand one's emotions and the emotions of others by one's third eye and to act appropriately on the basis of this understanding.**

Thus Emotional Quotient (EQ) is one's capacity to connect with other people and to experience satisfying relationship with them. Emotional Quotient gives us empathy, compassion, motivation and the ability to respond skillfully in any situation. Daniel Golé man an American behavioral scientist was the first man to write about EQ in 1995 in his book "Emotional Intelligence why it can matter more than IQ?"

Emotional intelligence is the outcome of the combination of uniform temperament, childhood experiences and latent learning, whereas Intelligence Quotient (IQ) is the measurement of one's intelligence based on knowledge and skills.

XIV.1. COMPONENTS OF EQ:

Self-Awareness: Knowledge of self is the first component of EQ. For better EQ one has to be fully aware of one's true nature, present feelings and being in touch with subtle or fleeting feelings about things.

Self-Motivation: Self-motivation is the second component of EQ. Motivations are of three types:

a. Motivation out of Fear: One motivates self to work on the basis of fear of losing one's jobs, or one's status in society or prestige etc. He will be motivated if some pressures are given. But this is short-lived motivation.

b. Motivation due to Incentives: One motivates oneself to work if one is given some incentive. Incentive may be increase in salary, out of turn promotions, bonus or overtime or appreciation etc. There is a limit of such types of incentives to work with more efforts or if incentives were given there may be limit of individuals, time or ones, inability to work for extra.

c. Self-Motivation: It is the best one and the real component of EQ because here one's involvement is by one's heart and soul. One becomes emotionally attached and gives one's best output. It can be understood with following examples:

There was a temple building work going on. Many people were working on the site. A person asked one worker what are you doing? The worker replied, "don't you see, I am carrying bricks". The person walked on and asked another worker the same question. That worker replied, "I am earning my bread and butter." The person walked on and asked yet another worker the same question. This worker replied, "I am carrying bricks to build temple of my lord".

You see here the three different replies to the same question. The first one shows **the involvement of only hand, the other shows the involvement of himself with his hand and head and third worker involved himself with head, hand and heart.** The third worker is involved emotionally and he is self-motivated he is putting his best effort.

Thus self-motivation requires a high level of optimism and persistence with involvement of heart despite dejection or obstruction. This will allow one to perform at peak level.

EMPATHY: Empathy involves reading and sensing unstated emotions and feelings of others even without being told. Someone with a strong sense of empathy often feels a rapport with people and interaction tends to go smoothly. **In a plain language empathy means you are able to sense others' feelings and emotions.** This is the most important component of emotional intelligence. People who have empathy are attuned to subtle ties in body language. They can hear the message beneath the words being spoken. Beyond that they have deep understanding of the existence and importance of cultural and ethnic difference.

EMOTIONAL MANAGEMENT: Emotional distress shrinks working memory and so diminishes the ability to think and imagine clearly. It inhibits intellect (the third eye) to function in the right direction. Being able to mange one's emotions will enable one to act rationally, and prevent any emotional outburst. Thus managing one's own emotion is important for two reasons:

a. People who are in control of their feelings and impulses are able to create an environment of trust and fairness.

b. People who have mastered their emotions are able to roll with the changes.

When a new change programme is announced, they do not panic, instead they are able to suspend judgements, see out information and listen to executive's explanations about new programme and then they are able to move with it.

SOCIAL EFFECTIVENESS: Social effectiveness means settling any disputes amicably and come out from a negotiation with a win–win situation.

Scientists feel that EQ is born largely in the neurotransmitters of the brain's limbic system, then governs feeling, impulses and drives. Their research indicates that the limbic system learns best through motivation, extended practice and feed back. On the other hand neocortex governs analytical and technical abilities. The neocortex grasps concepts and logic.

But here scientists studied and carried out research only on human's brain and its stimulation due to emotions or logic. They have ignored the "Being" aspect of human being. It is the Being of the living soul, which utilises these parts of human brain for logic and emotions. If more research is carried out on Being's emotions and its practical technique to raise EQ, it will be more fruitful.

CONSIDER THE FOLLOWING:

A few people are in a very happy mood and expressing their happy emotions by smiling and dancing in a marriage party. They are dancing because they are happy. At the same marriage party a person is just physically present but mentally upset. His presence is mere a formality. His sad emotions are due to his junior getting promotion and superseding him in his office. He is unable to manage his emotions and expresses his feelings of jealousy and anguish to anyone who meets him. He is unable to dance and enjoy because he is not happy.

Here, management of emotions is required practically. Here the high level of EQ is required which can make him to dance to be happy but dancing physically cannot be possible without the dance of intellect with its creative visualisation. The person with high level of EQ could have visualised the whole episode positively. He could have thanked heartily and accepted his superiority and at the same time he would have visualised of himself as being promoted in near future. He could have visualised himself performing better and start seeing himself as an effective employee to attract the due attention of the authority. He could have taken this as a challenge to his career and look this event as an opportunity to remove his shortcomings and improve his working ability, and this visualisation by his intellect can make him to dance physically and smile at any occasion. One needs not to search occasions to dance to express his happy feelings or feel happy because it is a happy occasion. One needs to be ever ready to change the mental picture (for visualisation) as and when required.

Thus the EQ is the ability to replace its mental picture of sad or unhappy emotions by positive mental picture (through creative visualisation) immediately to feel happy and joyful. This is called dance of intellect to feel happy or joyful.

Power of creative visualisation is the key to raise the level of EQ. And the enhanced level of EQ will certainly break the emotional barrier of Subconcious mind and will feel the Sub- concious mind with new mental positive picture to feel emotions of happiness and joy forever.

Thus higher level of EQ makes a man to dance intellectually to feel happy and joy forever rather than dancing physically because he is just happiness for a moment or on an occasion.

SO RAISE THE POWER OF POSITIVE VISUALISATION TO SEARCH THE HAPPINESS AND JOY WITHIN AND THUS RAISE THE LEVEL OF YOUR EQ

XV. THE POWERFUL THIRD EYE AND SPIRITUAL QUOTIENT (SQ)

The spiritual quotient is the ability of its own intellect to take right decision to uphold moral and ethical values despite stiff opposition. All problems of life are essentially spiritual problems and require a spiritual remedy. If one learns to recognise the spiritual roots of a problem, one can find more holistic and rewarding solutions to them by using spiritual intelligence. The lasting success and happiness cannot be achieved at the expense of morality. Because moral virtues are the original qualities of the soul and each deed that lessens these qualities leaves the soul more hollow. The soul exercises its own power of virtues by intellect's judgment capability.

Spiritual development is a systematic, methodic process that needs to be learnt and practised like any other skill. **Development of SQ raises the IQ with right knowledge and raises the level of EQ too with positive and realistic vision of life with moral values and divine virtues.** And thus SQ is the power to break all pseudo moral and pseudo ethical barriers of our Subconcious mind and activates the divine energy of our Subconcious mind to manifest divinity, which we already have. This is the crux of all religion.

Many people don't think about their spiritual lives until they are faced with a crisis such as a life threatening illness. Then they decide to embark on spiritual practices such as meditations or prayers. Consider the following questions if spirituality has been on your back burner for so long that you have forgotten that it is an essential part of being human.

Q1.   Why would you wait until you are about to die to focus on spirituality, when it could be enriching absolutely everything in your life today?

Q2.   How much are you prepared for dealing with life's greatest challenges (including death)?

Q3.   How will it be if you make a commitment right now to nourish your spirit in whatever way works best for you?

Q3.   How long are you going to keep depriving yourself of that which will bring you more satisfaction than anything the material world has to offer?

VISUALISE THE FOLLOWING:

Pretend you are going to die within 24 hours. What is most important to you: watching a sunset or sunrise, reading literature that gives you strength or perspective, communicating with nature, playing with your children or...

Whatever it is good enough for you when you are dying then it should certainly be important enough to pay attention to while you are alive.

Visualise about those times when people close to you were dying. What did they request at the end of their lives? Did they want to be near family members or personal mementoes? Did they crave for good, honest and heartful conversation? These are the kinds of things you want in your life, which will nourish you everyday. Live each day, as it is your last.

When the subject of spirituality comes up in conversation people often admit that they don't know what they believe. They have no idea about languages of their hearts. This can be a result of spiritual immaturity.

Perhaps long ago, they rejected their parent's religion or the kind of belief system that they felt was imposed upon them as children. Yet they have not taken the time or made the effort to seek out something that is more to their liking. These individuals are still mired in teenage rebellion or an ego-driven mode where they are too proud to even consider that their parents might have been wise about anything. These attitudes might be robbing them of possibilities for spiritual growth.

Develop a sense of maturity in your spiritual beliefs and practices that raise the level of SQ for becoming the best self-judge to break the barriers of caste, creed and orthodox barriers of religions.

XVI. THE THIRD EYE AND INACTIVE MEMORY

In order to activate our positive file from inactive memory and remain virtuous continually we must maintain soul-conscious state. The awareness that we are eternal soul with the original attributes of Truth, Peace, Love, Joy, Purity, Power and Bliss fills the mind with positivity and activate our positive file. If we are able to maintain this awareness with a powerful third eye, virtues will have their field day. In other words, the chain of Awareness – Thought – Decision – Action- Result becomes positive.

TABLE SHOWING HOW A POWERFUL THIRD EYE CAN ACTIVATE POSITIVE FILES FROM OUR MEMORY

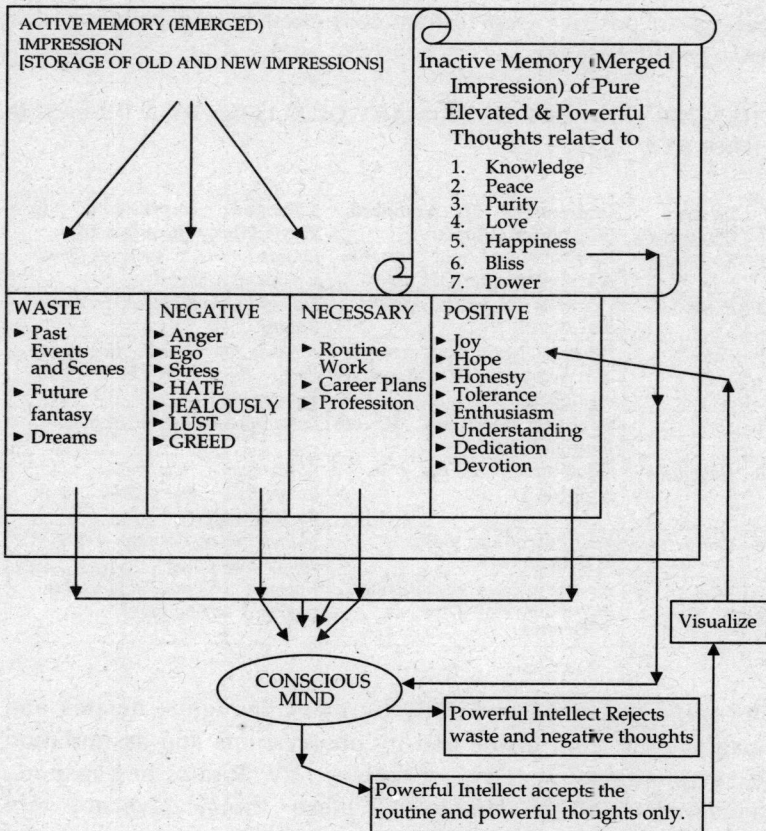

ACTIVE MEMORY (EMERGED) IMPRESSION
[STORAGE OF OLD AND NEW IMPRESSIONS]

Inactive Memory (Merged Impression) of Pure Elevated & Powerful Thoughts related to
1. Knowledge
2. Peace
3. Purity
4. Love
5. Happiness
6. Bliss
7. Power

WASTE	NEGATIVE	NECESSARY	POSITIVE
► Past Events and Scenes	► Anger	► Routine Work	► Joy
► Future fantasy	► Ego	► Career Plans	► Hope
► Dreams	► Stress	► Professiton	► Honesty
	► HATE		► Tolerance
	► JEALOUSLY		► Enthusiasm
	► LUST		► Understanding
	► GREED		► Dedication
			► Devotion

CONSCIOUS MIND

Visualize

Powerful Intellect Rejects waste and negative thoughts

Powerful Intellect accepts the routine and powerful thoughts only.

A powerful third eye can ensure that the positive chain is maintained. But a weak third eye lets the chain break and become negative.

At any moment, positive and negative thoughts arising from inactive and active memory respectively vie with each other for space on the screen of mind. Thoughts coloured by emotions alternate between fear and determination as propelled by the emerged impressions. The intellect fights to choose between the oscillating flow of thoughts. Finally when the intellect decides to act positively drawing on impressions of inactive memory with courage, victory is experienced with feelings of positive impressions continuously and positive files get opened forever.

CHANGED CONCEPT OF PRIMARY QUALITIES BY A DISEASED THIRD EYE

	Primary Qualities	Impressions in Standard File, which is inactive	Changed Impressions in Waste Files, which is active
1	Knowledge	Knowledge of Self, Supreme & Universal Eternal Cycle	Information of many fields known as General Knowledge
2	Purity	Purity of Thoughts, Speech and Action	External Cleanliness or External Beauty
3	Peace	Peace of Mind and absence of waste and negative thoughts.	Absence of Sound, Calm and Cool, Pin drop Silence in Environment
4	Love	Love for God and for all Human Being	Lust, Opposite Sex Attraction
5	Happiness	Contentment is the root of happiness.	Conditional happiness with Comfortable Life Style with Modern Gadgets
6	Power	Will Power and eight Spiritual Powers	Money Power, Position, status and Muscle Power
7	Bliss	Silence in trueconsciousness, beyond sense organs pleasures	Enjoying with sensual pleasures, involving sense organs.

Our mind is bombarded daily by many thoughts, desires and imaginations from inside and by observations and assimilation of surroundings, society, workplace, TV, Radio, newspapers, magazine etc. from outside. All these things have not only programmed our mind but increased the load of waste and negative files in our memory also. We need to deprogramme our waste and negative files and reprogramme it with positive images in order to trigger and activate standard files. Above table explains the changed concept of primary qualities which have changed our life style and created stress in every human being.

JUST CHECK YOUR THIRD EYE

Visualise that you have gone for a dinner party and there are lots of delicious dishes lying on the table. Now you take out the favourite one, keep on the plate, take a spoon, smell and feel that you are putting that in your mouth. Can you feel the saliva in your mouth?

This shows that your third eye is OK and you can make it powerful by practicing methods of visualisation.

16

IMPORTANCE OF MEMORY TECHNIQUES IN EDUCATION

The memory techniques are not a new idea. The ancient Greeks used it extensively. Mnemonics forms a large part of trained memory. The Greeks discovered that human memory is largely an association process that works by linking things together.

The main focus while making a mnemonic is for it to be illogical and humorous as this is easily remembered. The method is to note down all the key ideas or points of the chapter or any question, make a memorable sentence or word by taking all the first letters of each idea. This is the method of remembering using code words. Take for example, how we remember the different colours in rainbow: We use a code VIBGYOR for violet, indigo, blue, green, yellow, orange, red.

WHY MEMORY TECHNIQUES ARE IMPORTANT IN PRESENT EDUCATION SYSTEM?

A number of people remain skeptical about the potential of the human brain, pointing to the substandard performances that many of us routinely churn out. **Consider the following aspect of education, which is not given to students in the schools, colleges or universities.**

1. Brain, its function and memory power
2. Memory techniques
3. Function of mind
4. Difference between mind and brain
5. Application of study technique in day-to-day student life
6. How to develop concentration power

7.   How to motivate self.

8.   How to take examinations.

9.   The power of Third Eye for vivid visualisation.

10. How to develop creativity and so on.

The reason our performances do not match our potential is simply because we are given no information about what we are or about how we can best utilise our inherent qualities. Hence, understanding these basic concepts and techniques of memory will help us to match our performance with our inherent potential.

REMOVAL OF MENTAL BARRIERS TO BOOST THE PERFORMANCE OF STUDENTS

We have all seen an elephant tied down to a thin pole by an equally thin rope. Despite its size and strength the elephant doesn't break the chain and run away. This is because of a mental block. What happened was that when the elephant was only a baby, it was tied to a huge pole with very thick rope. The baby elephant, in spite of trying many times, could not break free and this eventually created a mental barrier in its mind that it couldn't run away no matter how hard it tried. As it grew, the thought became more and more ingrained in its mind and that is why it now stays wherever it has been tied down even though it has grown in size and strength and can break free.

To a large extent, we too are like that elephant, very powerful but unable to utilise our potential to the fullest. Hence one of the first steps to a good memory is to break down mental barriers.

One more scientist did an interesting experiment with fish. He took two fish and placed them in a vessel full of water. They were happily swimming all around the vessel. The scientist then kept a piece of glass in between the two fish in the middle of the vessel. As the fish swam, they came and hit the glass and could not go beyond it. After, some time, when the scientist removed the glass, he found that the fish were still not going beyond where the glass had been placed, despite the fact that it was no longer there. The fish still thought the piece of glass was there. This is the mental barrier, which the fish had created.

Similarly, another experiment was done with fleas in a jar. Fleas don't stay still for even a second. They keep jumping up and down, the person conducting this experiment placed a lid on top of this jar, after some time, when the lid was removed, the fleas did not jump out of the jar, instead, they were found jumping just short of the top because that was the extent to which they had been able to jump for significant length of time. And because they had become used to that height, they didn't jump any higher even when the lid was removed. It is this kind of restrictive thinking that is a huge obstacle on the road to success. To counter this, we need what is called "out of the box" or "creative" thinking. Let us illustrate this:

There was once a student who was very weak in mathematics and who often slept through the mathematics class. One day, the teacher warned him not to sleep but to pay attention in the class and come prepared with his homework the next day. As instructed, the boy tried but a few minutes into the class, he went to sleep. When he got up, the class was over and the teacher had left. All he remembered was that he had to come with his homework done. He looked around to see what it was that he had to do at home and found an algebra problem written on the blackboard. He copied it down and went home.

He sat late into the night trying to solve the problem because he didn't want to get scolded again. Finally, after another few hours of struggle, he managed to solve the problem. Next day, when he showed the solution to the teacher, the teacher was shocked. What had happened was that during class, the teacher had written on the blackboard an algebra problem to which no mathematician in the world had found a solution. And this boy, who was considered to be the dullest student in the class, had succeeded in one night. Even the cleverest student in the class had given up after trying a little or not trying at all.

The reason why this boy succeeded while others didn't was because he didn't know that this was an insolvable problem. The others had a mental barrier- if the world's greatest mathematicians had failed, how could schoolboys do any better? The dull boy didn't know what he was up against, did his best and came up with the answer.

So, in order to optimally use our brain, we need to be creative and think out of the box. Innovation and creativity are the twin keys to success in any field. And to be innovative and creative, one needs to break free of mental barriers.

17

FACTORS AFFECTING OUR MEMORY

It is said that "memory is the treasury and guardian of all things." Cognitive psychologists say that memories are not duplicate impressions of earlier events, but reconstructions of earlier events.

Just have a glance at the following series of letters:

O I C U R M T

Glance at the letters again. This time close your eyes almost immediately. You will notice that is an afterimage of the shapes. Even though the afterimage lasts only for an instant – a second at most - it plays a role in the memory process. Immediately after you see hear, or feel something, there is a fragile, brief lingering of the perception.

By finding patterns, looks, images, associations, and meanings, memories become richer and more accessible. Author Linda Perigo Moore has said, "it is not how you take it out, it is how you put it in."

If you tried to find a hook, a pattern, another meaning, you may recognise that the sounds of the letters, O I C U R M T, form the phrase, "OH, I SEE YOU ARE EMPTY". Once you know this, letters are easy to recall.

There are following factors that often affect our memory in day-to-day life:

A. EXTERNAL MEMORY AIDS

External memory aids include such strategies as:

Taking notes

- Making shopping lists
- Entering appointments in a diary or in a calendar.
- Writing a memo to self
- Writing on the back of your hand
- Using clocks, timers, alarms on watches, computers, mobile phones, planners etc.
- Putting objects in a conspicuous place
- Putting a knot in your handkerchief
- Asking someone to help you remember

Making lists or writing reminder notes to self are the most widespread external memory aids. It seems that list making is primarily helpful as a way of organising information rather than its more obvious role in retrieving.

WHEN TO USE EXTERNAL MEMORY AIDS?

1. When a number of interfering activities occur between encoding and recall, such as having to remember to buy groceries after work.

2. Need to make doctor's appointment two months in advance (having a long time between encoding and recall.)

3. When internal aids are not trusted to be sufficiently reliable (i.e. when precise details are to be remembered)

4. When there is insufficient time to properly encode the information.

5. When memory load is to be avoided (i.e. when you have to attend to more than one activity at one time.)
How effective are these External Memory Aids?

In general, external aids are regarded easier to use, more accurate and more dependable than mental strategies.

However, with the exception of note taking, there has been research into the effectiveness of external memory aids.

One problem with external aids is that most of them are highly specific in their use. Their effective use also requires good habits. It is no good remembering to make a note in your diary, if you don't remember to look at it.

B. INTERNAL MEMORY TECHNIQUES:

There are situations where list making appears appropriate but is not, in fact, the best strategy. For example, the waiter in a hotel who went from table to table to take drink orders would be much better at remembering the orders if he visualised the drinks in particular locations rather than when he wrote the orders down. It is perhaps the time pressure in that kind of situation that makes an internal strategy more effective than an external one.

WHEN TO USE INTERNAL TECHNIQUES?

1. When you can't rely on external prompts (acting in a drama etc.)

2. When external prompts are difficult to prepare or hard to use.

3. When you don't expect the need to recall something and have nothing prepared.

4. When using external aids interferes with other behaviour (understanding what's going on, taking orders etc.)

5. When carrying external aids would be undesirable or inconvenient (while driving etc.)

6. When the interval between learning and recall is very short (as when you need to remember a phone number only long enough to dial it.)

There are various internal memory methods which one can practice to remember different kinds of information. These techniques are explained in the subsequent chapters.

C. RECENCY AND PRIMACY EFFECT:

Dozens of studies have prove the existence of the "Recency effect' and the "Primacy effect'. Primacy means that you tend to have better recall for things that happen at the beginning of an event or situation. Recency means that you tend to remember things that happened most recently.

D. Similarity Effect:

It is easier to remember a variety of things if you group them together. By grouping, you will be able to recall much more information than you would normally be able to.

Try it for yourself. Here is a list of 20 words. Look quickly at each once, then cover up the list and see how many you can remember.

1.	Lotus	11.	Aeroplane
2.	Lion	12.	Curd
3.	Table	13.	Tulip
4.	Car	14.	Chair
5.	Rice	15.	Deer
6.	Rabbit	16.	Daffodil
7.	Rose	17.	Bed
8.	Motor cycle	18.	Train
9.	Desk	19.	Vegetables
10.	Sambhar	20.	Kangaroo

However, if you classify them in some broad headings, it becomes very easy to remember.

Flowers	Vehicles	Food	Furniture	Animal
Lotus	Car	Rice	Table	Lion
Rose	Motorcycle	Sambhar	Chair	Rabbit
Tulip	Truck	Curd	Desk	Deer
Daffodils	Aeroplane	Vegetables	Bed	Kangaroo

See how simple it is? Once you organise the list, you need to remember only five categories and only four items in each category. Each is within the comfort level for your short-term memory and well below the uncomfortable maximum. The same basic theory can have a dramatic effect on how much you will remember for a test.

E. INTENSITY:

The factor that makes sensory and emotional associations work so well in memory is their intensity. The more intense the feeling, Colour, smell, pain or joy, the more likely you are never to forget it. It creates strong impressions very quickly and its uniqueness makes it easy to recall.

F. WEIRDNESS EFFECT:

You are more likely to remember things that are unusual, outrageous or out of place. In the list of 20 words we had above, if we add words such as Zulu or Zoroastrian or Ninja, we will be able to remember them better. The reason is that the words are very different. They stand out and that makes them memorable. Adding a "weirdness" element to the things you are trying to memorise will increase the limits of your memory.

WHY DO YOU FORGET? :

LACK OF ATTENTION: If we haven't paid proper attention to anything we want to remember, it forms only a weak impression on our memory. Attention can be defined as directing mental activity towards a mental or physical object or situation. Attention is to the mind what lens focus is to a camera. In the absence of attention, our brain does not get a clear impression of an object or situation. In the absence of a clear impression, there can be no clear memory to recall either.

USE OR LOSE: Believe it or not, an average human being loses up to 100000 brain cells every day due to disuse. Unlike the other cells of our body, brain cells do not multiply. Any cells that are damaged or not used simply degenerate and die. By the age of 35, a human being loses over 1000 nerve cells every day.

LACK OF MENTAL EXERCISE: The less a person uses his brain, the worse his memory becomes. People get mentally out of shape when they stop challenging their minds. This happens when they opt for habitual solutions rather than purposeful thought, or if they confine their thinking to a small range of interests. Remember that mental fitness - your ability to concentrate, to reason, to visualize, to imagine, to make decisions, to solve problems, and to think creatively depends greatly on how well and how often you exercise your mind. You need to exercise all of your mental muscles in order to keep yourself mentally fit. Just like several body muscles work together to create physical movement, mental muscles work together to create clear purposeful thinking.

INTERFERENCE: Other activities we pursue after learning something also interfere with our ability to remember.

REPRESSION: Unconscious forgetting of painful memories is known as 'repression'. For example, people often forget an appointment with the dentist and but not with their girl/boyfriend. It is a fact that pleasant experiences are recalled more easily than unpleasant ones. Often, one tends to forget the list of provisions they were asked to buy but not the address of their girl/boyfriend.

SHOCKS: These are of two types: intense emotional experiences of a distressing nature, or a shock given for mental illness. Even when somebody suffers an accident, injury or trauma, or witnesses some unbelievable incident, one tend to block it out of one's memory.

DRUGS: Taking a variety of medicines for various diseases can also affect memory. Further, drugs like marijuana, a brown sugar and other drugs, alcohol and tobacco also damage the faculty of memory.

FACTORS CONTRIBUTING FOR A BETTER MEMORY

A.Strong Impression: At any given time, various impressions converge upon the mind. When the impression is stronger, the memory recall will be that much easier and faster. Memory basically has three aspects: Registration, Retention and Recall. If the registration is good, the impression formed will also be stronger. For stronger impressions, you need to involve all your five senses: hear, smell, taste, touch and sight as any input to the brain only goes through these five senses. When more than one sense is involved, the impressions are stronger.

For example: Next time, when you put down your house keys or car keys, consciously experience setting them down, rather than just dropping them off thoughtlessly. If you place them on a table, look around you. See the surface on which the keys are resting. Ask yourself is it dark or light? Is it smooth or rough? Is it high or low or somewhere in between? Look at the keys. Are they lying fanned out or piled on top of each other? Is the key ring lying flat or at an angle? Picture the keys in your mind. Touch the keys and the surface. What do they feel like? Engage all your senses. Can you smell anything? Is the air warm or cool? You never know what cue may trigger your recollection. In the beginning, it may take several seconds to build up your impression. Later it takes an instant.

B. Concentration: Our attention is constantly shifting. Develop the habit of reining in your mind every time it wanders to other things. A quiet mind is the best guarantee of concentration. Concentration automatically means a stronger impression.

C. Habit: Concentration is a habit and habits are perfected by practice. We must persevere in trying to concentrate until we succeed. Habit is as strong a force for good as for evil. We should try to build up habits that are conducive to concentration.

D. Interest: The law of interest is of paramount importance in concentration and thereby for improved memory. Things, which we are deeply interested in, are remembered without conscious effort. Throw your heart and soul into a thing, make it vital for yourself; you cannot forget anything that is vital to you.

CREATING INTEREST IS THE KEY FOR REMEMBERING.

There are some subjects, which we remember accurately, and we remember not only the lesson but also very often the way in which it was presented, the voice of the teacher, his instructions and examples, and sometimes even the answer given by our classmates.

And what are just stated for schools holds true for everyday life, business or social. For instance there is one day of a certain holiday, which still stands out clearly in our mind while the rest of the holidays are shrouded in fog. There is one conversation with Miss Tina of which we remember every word; and there are hundred other conversations, most of them more recent, more important, more significant and yet their content is entirely forgotten. Why?

Of course there is an answer. IT IS INTEREST, which compels us to give undivided attention to a certain object and to concentrate on it to the exclusion of other thoughts that might interfere. Even if you are not interested, improve your concentration by strengthening your interest. Study a subject because you think it is worth studying and not simply because you have to. The basic reason why students don't remember what they read is because they have no interests in their studies. When you have clear-cut goals and know how studying and remembering these subjects is going to help you achieve your goals. Then you will automatically develop an interest.

E. Relaxation: Concentration occurs most naturally when both the body and the mind are relaxed. Sit down in a relaxed posture. This helps in enhancing memory power. Take five deep breaths. As you exhale, say to your self relax, relax and relax. Automatically you will find your mental condition improving.

F. Solution of Emotional Conflicts: When you are emotionally upset or worried, you cannot concentrate on anything, reading disabilities occur mostly when we are dealing with emotional difficulties as well. It is not lack of concentration, it is some other problem not connected with the subject to be studied. Emotional stress stemming from problems like a family dispute, problems in one's marriage, problems with one's boss, etc, all lead to lack of concentration. It has to be resolved for a better memory.

G. Repetition: Repetition facilitates comprehension and aids memory. Resolve to remember even by repetition. But remember, mere repetition does not ensure good memory.

H. Attention: People tend to remember what is relevant to them. That is why a fashion designer can easily remember shades of colour, why an international banker can recite exchange rates, and why an astronomer can instantly recognise star patterns. In each case the subject holds meaning for them. Because we remember what is important to us, we can enhance our memory by deciding whether something is, in fact, important. If it is important we naturally pay more attention. We give ourselves the motivation to recall.

It is true that we cannot always decide beforehand how important something will be, or whether something will be worth remembering. But at times we can judge whether we will need some information in the future. Here are three ways to help you decide.

1. ASK YOURSELF, "What would happen if I dcn't remember this? Would it really make any difference?" If it wouldn't then don't bother remembering it.

2. ASK YOURSELF, "How soon do I need to use this information?" If you need it sooner, then it has the greatest impact.

3. ASK YOURSELF, "Does anything else depend on remembering this information?" A subject's real importance is measured by its value related to other subjects.

In the process of deciding whether something is worth remembering, you determine its importance. If you think something makes a real difference to you and other people, if it carries immediate impact, it takes the top of the list. Giving a piece of information a high priority automatically encourages you to pay more attention. To keep your memory muscles in shape, it is helpful to develop the habit of paying close attention

I. Recalling Exercises: CAN YOU RECALL:

What were you thinking about five minutes ago?
What were you thinking about an hour ago?
What were you doing yesterday at this time?
What you had for breakfast for the last three days?
What did you wear on three days ago?
What are some of your earliest memor.es?
What are some of your most vivid memories?
What are some of your dimmest memcries?
What kind of things do you have a good memory for?
What kind of things do you have a poor memory for?

Sit across from another person, select a sentence at random from a book, and read it to yourself. Look the other person in the eyes, and recite the sentence exactly; the other person then repeats what you said. If he or she makes a mistake, repeat the sentence. When the person repeats the sentence correctly, move on to another. Choose short sentences and gradually move to longer and more difficult sentences. After a while switch roles.

Recall Your Dinner Picture: Next time if you have dinner at a restaurant, take a mental snapshot of what your place setting looks like. Do this by visualizing an imaginary connection between one object on the table and another. For Example The salt shaker falls onto the dinner plate, which in turn spins, causing the fork and knife on the plate to strike the glass, causing the vase to tumble, making the six flowers land on the water glass, and so on.

Recall something you told yourself that you would never forget.

Daily Recalling Exercises: When you go to bed at night, before drifting off to sleep, visualize the day's events. Picture what happened to you, starting from the moment you awoke. Visualize what your life would look like if a hidden camera were following you around all day. As you go to sleep, recall all that you heard throughout the day. Do the same for what you smelled, what you tasted, and what sensations you experienced.

J. Will power: Choose a simple action such as tying your shoes, scratching your nose, or stretching your legs, and decide that you will perform this action at a certain time later today. For example, decide that at 6 pm you will clean your glasses. What might make you forget to do this? You can develop the will power for a better memory in very simple way. These simple activities certainly contribute to our memory power.

Memory gives us a sense of personal continuity and direction. Our everyday thoughts include plans, expectations, and recollections, which frame a sense of context. Expectations and plans seem to be located ahead of the present. We mentally gaze forward, as if we were traveling to this destination.

But these impressions are just a way of indexing our experience. All our experiences take place in the present moment. Each and every thought – those that refer to future events- as also those that refer to past events- is expected in real time.

18

STAGES AND LAWS OF MEMORY TECHNIQUES

There are three stages by which a clear memory is formed. These are Registration, Retention & Recollection.

1.Registration: Formation of memory begins with registering the information during perception by sense organs. The data is then filed in a short-term memory system, which is very limited. At this stage sense organs have to be alert for registering the information clearly. Otherwise, the waste and negative information, which keep coming from subconscious or unconscious memory, might replace it soon.

2. Retention: The process of storing the perceived information for longer duration is called Retention. This process involves the third eye's visual imagery, association with words or images that are related to something they already know because there is already a file in their memory related to that information, or other experiences such as smell or sounds. Periodical revision plan is very necessary for retaining the information for longer duration.

3. Recollection: The final stage of memory is recollection, in which information stored in memory is brought up into the conscious mind when it is required. This further depends on the state of mind. Alpha state of mind helps to recall the full information stored in the memory bank.

LAWS OF MEMORY TECHNIQUES

There are following laws of memory techniques:

1. The law of Comprehension: The better we understand, the

better we learn, i.e., material is better retained if we have understood it. Comprehend the numbers- 58121519222629. This set of numbers is based on the principle of adding 3 & 4.

2. The law of spaced learning: Spacing out learning over several days is better than material amassed on one day. Daily practice should be the rule. Driving an hour daily for 10 days is much more fruitful than driving for 10 hours on a single day.

3. The law of recitation: Instead of re-reading, recite to yourself what you have learnt. Interrupt your reading and mentally recapitulate the main points. Reading aloud has several advantages such as:

a. It improves pronunciation.
b. It utilises the ear – auditory memory.
c. Your work becomes more interesting.

Reading over and over again is not the best method of study. It uses only the eyes. Read aloud and try to discuss what you are studying with another person.

4. The law of Over Learning: Whatever you want to remember, say it over and over again to yourself both silently and out loud. Adopt the habit of frequently revising the material you have learned. Go over your lessons several times.

5. The law of Whole Learning: Learn the material as a whole rather than bit by bit. Repeat it as a whole over and over again. Long passages should be divided into meaningful sections. Learn a poem as a whole rather than one stanza at a time. This adds meaning to learning and becomes easier to memorize.

6. The law of Confidence: Your poor memory is fallout of the fact that you keep telling yourself that your memory is poor. An attitude of confidence with regard to one's memory

tends to make it better, rather than repeating to you, "my memory is improving." It would be better to learn the various memory techniques. The best way to boost your confidence is to register and reproduce random numbers by applying these techniques. Never abuse your memory by giving it a bad name. Get acquainted with your memory and make friends with it. Treat it well and it will serve you well.

7. The law of Re-Integration: We remember better if certain conditions present at the time of learning are also present when we try to remember what we have learned. When the original conditions of learning are reinstated, remembering is enhanced. For example - a foreign language is best learned by living in a country where it is spoken widely.

8. The law of Figure and Ground: Anything is remembered better if it contrasts with its background. Take for instance, words in italics or underlined. These are remembered better than normal text since they stand out. Playing music in the background to calm one's nerves and remove other distractions also helps people trying to concentrate and memorize important things.

9. The law of Association: Association plays a vital role in creative memory. The mind has a tendency to associate the new material to the old ones that were similar. Given below are some instances from a simple word association game that children often play for amusement.

Call word	Response
Son	Father
Party	Celebration
Examination	Study
Gavaskar	Cricketer
Good	Bad

19

PROCESS OF REGISTRATION IN OUR MEMORY

There are two methods of registration of any information in our memory bank.
These are as follow:

A. General method: The general method is related to day-to-day observations by the sense organs and reciting for registering the information or the images.

B. Short cut method: The short cut method involves using the mind languages, creating memory triggers and visualising with IBMC techniques. IBMC means:

I – I, me, myself (you should see yourself)

B – Big

M – Moving (in action)

C – Colour

The picture that you visualise should include you i.e. you should be able to see yourself in action in your imagination. Secondly it should be a big, huge and enormous picture. Thirdly, the picture should not be a still photograph, but a movie in action means it should be moving picture and lastly it should have colours, as this will make it retentive.

CREATING MEMORY TRIGGERS FOR REGISTRATION

Memory triggers are created by various memory techniques as follows:

I. MNEMONIC TECHNIQUES OF ASSOCIATION

Mnemonic techniques are the basic tools for registration in our memory. It is also for improving our retention and recollection from our memory. Named after Mnemosyne, the Greek Goddess of memory, mnemonic techniques are simple methods to develop the memory power. They include unusual ways of memorizing huge amounts of information. A number of different techniques are used to associate something with something that we already know. For example First letter cueing, acronyms, acrostics, popular saying etc.

These techniques were of almost unbelievable importance hundreds of years ago before the invention of printing presses. Most of the people did not have access to pens and paper or printed materials that time. Relying on their own memories was the way of paramount importance. Indeed, for the ancient Greeks and Romans, mnemonic techniques are one of the most important subjects taught in classical schools. They were often used by the Great Orators of the time to remember their speeches. Without these techniques their tasks would have been impossible.

Mnemonic technique is not only just a trick, but also a serious method to help us paying attention, registering information, retaining and recalling information from our memory. Since this is a method, we need to practice them over and over in order to become comfortable with using them everyday. These techniques don't rely on magic but on our own ability to visualise, making connections or associations and organising important information.

First letter Cueing: One of the easiest ways to remember a string of words is to use first-letter cueing, in which the first letter of a word is used as a cue to remember the word itself. For example:

a. How many planets are there in our solar system?
You can remember the sentences: My Very Educated Mother Just Showed Us Nine Planets, which stand for Mercury, Venus, Earth, Mars, Jupiter, Saturn, Uranus, Neptune and Pluto.

b. In mathematics we have the rule of BODMAS: Brackets, Off, Divide, Multiplication, Addition and Subtraction.

Acronyms: First-letter cueing usually employs acronyms (making a word or words out of the first letters of the words to be remembered). Many organisations and governmental bodies use acronyms. For example ISRO stands for Indian Space Research Organisation. Some acronyms become so familiar that we forget what the letter stands for. For example LASER, which is acronym for Light Amplification by Stimulated Emission of Radiation. ASH: Action on Smoking & Health and SEA:Shipbuilding Exports Association.

Acrostics: A related form of the first letter cueing is the acrostic, in which the first letter in a series of words, lines, or verses from the information to be remembered. For example The trigonometry formulae for Sin, Cos, Tangent is mostly known as PANDIT BADRI PRASAD HAR HAR BOLE, SONA CHANDI TOLE.

The only problem with acronym or acrostics is the tendency to forget the system we devise. To remove this possibility, try making a visual association with the short cut. In above example we can visualise a Panditjee named Badri Prasad is praying by telling HAR HAR and after that weighing gold and silver to donate.

Popular sayings/creating associated images: whether or not we realize it, each of us uses some of these techniques all the time. For example:

1. She was all gay (ALGAE) and he was a fun guy (FUNGI). They took a likin (LICHEN) to each other is a mnemonic to remember that LICHEN are made up of ALGAE and FUNGI.

2. Can Intelligence Karen Solve Some Foreign Mafia Operations? Is an excellent mnemonics to remember the Krebs Cycles: Citric Acid, Isocitric, Ketoglutaric, Succinyl, Succinic, Fumaric, Malic and Oxaloacetic.

3. For spelling and grammar, here are mnemonics to help you get over same confusion:

* "A FRIEND is always there when the END comes" for people who always look at "Friend" and wonder whether it is spelt "Friend" or "friend'.

* George eats old gray rats and paints houses yellow is for how to spell "Geography".

* A Rat In The House Might Eat The Ice Cream: the first letter of each word put together spell Arithmetic.

* The word "Believe" has a "Lie" in it. : To help solve the "Ie" or 'ei' problem.

* Your principal is your PAL. : The difference between principle (A rule) and Principal (head of a school).

* RAVEN: RAVEN is the rule to help Remember that Affect is a verb but Effect is a noun.

* When you assume something, you make an "ass" of "u' and "Me" - This is how you spell "assume'. It is also a great reminder to avoid assumptions.

* Business or Business: - connect Bus and Business – use a single S.

* Tomorrow or Tomorrow? : Tom will come tomorrow – use a single M.

* Dessert or Desert? : Dessert is so sweet- uses two S's. But the desert is full of sand, use one S.

* Stationery or Stationary? : Stationary has an "a" in the second last syllable, as in standing still. So the one with the "e" must refer to paper etc.

* Metre or Meter: Metre is the unit of measuring length in the metric system. And "Metre' contains the letters "TR" just like in "Metric". Now 'Meter" is the measuring device and is therefore spelt the other way.

4. Hyper or Hypo: Hyper means over as in the fairly familiar words

Hyperactive: – Excessively or abnormally active.
Hyperbole: Exaggerated speech.
Hypercritical: Over critical, especially in trivial matters.
Hyperextension: Extension of a limb beyond the normal range of movement.
Hyper market: A very large super market with a greater range of goods.
Hyper sensitive: Over sensitive.
Hyper space: Where there exist more than three dimensions.
Hyper tension: High blood pressure.

5. Hypo means under or beneath, as in:
Hypocrisy: Insincerity, falsehood (Less than the truth).
Hypochondria: Neurotic conviction of illness.
Hypodermic:Beneath the skin.
Hypoglycemia: Low blood sugar.
Hypothesis; - A proposition stated as a basis for argument or reasoning, lacking proof.
Hypoxia: Oxygen deficiency in the tissues.

6. Eat an Aspirin after a Night time Snack: The 7 continents (note: the second letter in the first three "a" words help to remember the A continents) Europe, Antarctica, Asia, Africa, Australia, North America, south America.

7. HOMES: To remember the Great Lakes in America: Huron, Ontario, Michigan, Erie, Superior.

8. In 1903 the Wright Brothers flew free:The rhyme helps remember the year of the first successful flight.

9. Divorced, Beheaded, Died; Divorced, Beheaded, and Survived:A very commonly heard mnemonic for the fate of the six wives of King Henry VIII.

10. Sober Physicists Don't Find Giraffes In Kitchens: The orbital names for electrons (SPDFGIK).

11. Kipper Hardly Dare Move During Cold Months: Descending order of Metric Scale: Kilo, Hecto, Deca, Metre, Deci, Centi, and Mili.

12. A quick brown fox jumps over the black lazy dog: To type every letter of the alphabet in one sentence.

13. Counting the number of letters in each word of "May I have a large container of coffee?" gives you the value of "Pi" to the 7th place (3.1415926).

14. The phrase "How I wish I could calculate" gives the value of "Pi" up to five places (3.14159)

II. MNEMONIC STRATEGY OF LOCI SYSTEM

The oldest known mnemonic strategy (it dates to 500 B.C.) is the method of Loci. Loci are the plural of Locus, which means place or location. The loci system was used as a memory tool by both Greek and Roman orators, who took advantage of the technique to speak without notes. They would visualise objects that represented the topics they wanted to discuss, and then mentally place the objects in different locations within a building. As an orator spoke, he would mentally move through the building, retrieving the imaginary objects from each location as he came to it. This ancient oratorical method is the origin of our idiom "in the first place." The method of loci was the most popular mnemonic system until about the middle of the 1600s, when other strategies (such as the phonetic and peg systems) were introduced.

This method is based on the assumption that people best remember familiar locations. Therefore, these locations can serve as clues to help in remembering information associated with them. To use the method of loci effectively, all we have to do is linking something we want to remember with a location. When we want to recall the information, we simply remember the location.

STEPS OF LOCI SYSTEM:

First, choose a place we know well, such as our house.

Secondly, visualise a series of locations in that place in a logical order. For example Begin at the front door, go through the hall, turn into the living room, proceed through the dining room and then into the kitchen. As we enter each location, always move logically and consistently in the same direction, from one side of the room around to the others. Each piece of furniture or architectural elements of the house can serve as an additional location.

Thirdly, associate each piece of information in the order it is to be remembered with a particular location in the house and visualise the association.

For example: Remember following items:

Paper, carrots, ice cream, rice, edible oils.

Visualise the front door is covered with the paper and now enter into the hall and see the hall is full of carrots and you are eating the tasty carrots. Now enter into the living room and see you are offered an ice cream and you taste the ice cream. Now enter into the dining room where your guests are feasting on rice and finally you moved into the kitchen where you slipped on spread edible oils on floor.

This method can be used for a variety of lists, for speeches, names, and things to do, even to remember a thought we want to keep in our mind. The loci system works so well because it alters the way we remember. It allows us to use familiar locations to cue ourselves about things we want to recall. Because the locations are organised in a natural order, one memory easily leads into the next, dragging with it whatever information we have attached to the location.

We can enlarge the system by adding other buildings we know well. For example: our school, office building, store, parent's house, in-laws house etc. We could easily walk through a neighbor-hood, or visualise our garden. It is also possible to add more than one item to any location. For example: if we want to remember a list of 50 items to be purchased at the store, we could theoretically place 5 items at each of 10 locations with mnemonic strategy of association.

MEMORISING SPEECH BY LOCI SYSTEM

Most of the time you are scrutinized and continuously watched during the examination period. It is done just to ensure that during the examination you are not using any unfair means. All this leads to extra pressure and it is seen that under such situations you tend to forget or your memory doesn't work properly. To get going in such trying conditions and that too in front of your teacher's eyes, you will have to use the 'Loci System' to cheat the teacher. This will help you recall the answer on the spot.

This method is a boon for all those who are invited to the stage for a speech and cannot afford to carry the written speech with them. They are not able to perform fully and have to sacrifice eye-to-eye contact with the audience in case of delivering a speech without preparations. They have to face a great deal of embarrassment at times when they forget their speech on table or when they miss some point during speech. By using cheating method your speech w ll be perfectly all right and while delivering it you will be able to express yourself fully through your hand movements, gestures and eye-to-eye contact with the audience. This will not only impress organisers and audience alike but will instill a great confidence in you that will give birth to a great orator in you.

You have to have a very attentive look a: the venue of your speech or examination hall. You have to associate all the keywords of your speech to these objects and while you are speaking, instead of a written speech, you have to look at all the objects and surroundings. At the same time you have to give an indication, while speaking, to the various directions of objects and that's all. You will complete your speech very comfortably and because of your way of deliverance, you will earn accolades from one and all. I will explain it by an example of my friend Mr Biswaroop Roy Choudhary, who is a Limca book record holder as India's strongest memory man.

When he goes for a seminar for memory demonstration inside the seminar hall, he comes across many objects such as fans, table, projector, audience, chairs, screen, air conditioner, sofa set, marker, flower pot, door, windows, dining hall, utensils and parking place of cars, bikes and trees (which are outside the seminar hall) etc. These objects help to instantly prepare a speech. For example: if he has to deliver a speech on characteristics of a good leader. he asks his audience to give him some points about the subject i.e. characteristics of a Good leader. Some of the suggestions that he gets are like this. A good leader should have:

Vision
Intelligence
Responsibility
Knowledge
Health
Followers

Commanding-ability
Good speaking ability
Learned person
Charismatic appearance -

While linking or associating each point with these objects he would look at them very carefully and once again, when he finishes association, he would repeat the process.

He just memorizes these points but at the same time he would link each of them with above-mentioned objects in following way by creating his own Personalized Meaning System (PMS):

Characteristics	PMS	Association
1. Vision	Vision	Projector (A good projector has a good vision).
2. Intelligent	Intelligent student	Chair (intelligent students sit on Chairs).
3. Responsibility	Rush with sponge	Table (People are rushing to clean table with sponge).
4. Knowledge	Nal (tap) at edge	Windows (nal/tap is fitted to the edge of window).
5. Healthy	See exercise	Door (A person is exercising near the door).
6. Followers	Following	Air conditioner (People are following each other and standing near Air Conditioner to get cool air).
7. Commanding ability	Come & mend	Parking (A man is shouting at the parking to come and mend the cars).
8. Good speaking ability	Speakers	Fans (Big and good speakers are fitted to fans).
9. Learned personality	Learning lessons	Sofa set (A person is sitting on Sofa and learning lessons).
10. Charismatic appearance	Karishma Kapoor	Tree (Karishma Kapoor is sitting on a tree).

Thus after preparing the speech he delivers it with full confidence. After salutation he starts his speech in the following manner.

While looking at projector he says that a good leader should be a good visionary. Then he looks at chair and says he should be intelligent as well and by looking towards table he says that a leader should be a responsible person. In this way people who are sitting near table will feel addressed and taken care of.

Throughout his speech he will look towards all the objects and carry on with his speech without forgetting any point. Knowledgeable (window), healthy (Door), followers

(A.C), commanding ability (Parking), (here because parking is outside the hall and as he mentions it through movement of his eyes and hands, people sitting at the last rows also would feel addressed), good speaker (Fans), learned personality (Sofa sets), charismatic (Tree). In this way he would look at different directions for recollection with the help of memory triggers, which were instantly prepared, and delivers the speech successfully. Audiences also feel satisfied.

This method can be replicated in the examination hall, as students can find many objects and can link the points of their answers during or before the start of exams. According to the feed back of almost thousands of people, this method has helped them and their performance has enhanced dramatically. Many of the poor students have passed their exams with good marks and have enormous self-confidence now. Initially they hated exams but now they wait for it eagerly.

This method is also known as 'JOURNEY METHOD', where you can fix say 25 points in your journey from your house to some place say market or cinema theatre. When you learn an answer you can associate each of its points to one of the stops. Since you already know the stops, you will be able to recollect the answer faster and with accuracy.

III. MEMORY TECHNIQUE OF THE LINK METHOD

The link method, also known as the chain system, is the most basic of the mnemonic strategies. It is used for memorizing short lists of items, such as a shopping list, in which each item is linked to the next. Here is how to perform the link system:

1. Form a visual image for each item in the list.

2. Associate the image for the first item with the image for the second item.

3. Associate the image for the third item with the image for the second item and so on.

4. Begin with the first item and proceed in order as each item leads to the next one to recall the lists.

It is important not to try to associate every item with every other item. Instead, we are just associating the two items at a time. While creating visual association, we must see vividly by our third eye. Although a funny or unusual association is good, what is most important is that we use the first association that comes to our mind, since this will make it easier for us to remember the same association.

SOME TIPS ON THE IMAGE MAKING IN THE LINK SYSTEM INCLUDE:

1. Make images involving you and make predominantly visual images but try to involve all senses. We carry out visualisation through our senses of seeing, hearing, touch, taste and smell and also involve action or movement. One should use visualisation to check on the state of one's imaginative memory as follow:

Hearing: With eyes closed, one can visualise the wind producing musical notes.

Sight: With eyes closed one can visualise that the kite is flying in the sky. It climbs up and then falls. It is dark blue in colour, flying high up in the sky and it looks tiny.

Touch: Visualise you are holding a chilled soft drink bottle and feel the chilling sensation.

Taste: Visualise you are sitting in a restaurant and being served a sumptuous meal.

Movement: Think you are pacing up and down in a park. The grass there is wet and you are pacing briskly. But all this while you have got to keep yourself relaxed so that the imaginative skills are retained and not lost.

2. Make solid images of abstract ideas.

3. Make simple and logical sequences but exaggerate the sizes and distort the features to the point of absurdity of the objects involved so that they become easy to remember.

4. Use humorous and colourful images.

5. Use hyperbole: In order to reproduce a number of words from a memory in a particular sequence, experts recommend use of hyperbole (exaggeration), multiplications, substitutions etc.

6. Visualise your mental pictures to be too large and out of proportion to the objects size. For example, think of a needle, which is a metre long, surprised? But there is no harm in thinking so. After all you have not to pay for visualising things. Next, think of a fountain pen that is as large as a tree.

7. Substitute your items, it is simply thinking of another item instead of the earlier one. Supposing you want to memorise two items, a birthday cake and a book.

8. Visualise the cake is rectangular. Try to cut it. The knife does not pass through. Examine closely. It is a book with a cover like chocolate.

   To sum up we can say that Visualise things in action, out of proportion, illogically, colourful, in 3-dimension and use all your senses to get it impressed in the memory.

THE LIMITATION OF LINKS

We may have already spotted one of the problems with this system – each item is linked to the previous one, except for the very first item. We will need to think of some way to cue that first item. If the list is a shopping list, try linking the first item with the entryway to the store. If somebody else gave the list to you, link the first item with that person.

It is also possible that if we forget one item on the linked list, the item that it is linked with next may also be forgotten. The method of loci has an advantage over the link system in that even if one item is forgotten, it will not affect memory for the next item, because all of the items are linked to an unforgettable place, not to each other.

Both the link and loci methods can be used to remember items in order. However, neither of these memory techniques allows us to locate just one particular item on the list. For example: if we wanted to find the tenth item on our list, in the link system we would have to work our way through the first nine items in our list to get it. Likewise, in the loci method, we would have to walk through our house step by step until we arrived at the tenth item. On the other hand, this weakness is true of most lists that we have thoroughly learned in a serial way. It is much easier to recite the letters of the alphabet in order than to name them all in a random sequence.

Aware of this, the ancients did come up with one way around it when using the method of loci. Every so often, say every fifth location – place a distinguishing mark. At the fifth location, for example: picture a five-dollar bill. At the tenth location, visualise a clock with its hands pointing to ten o' clock. This way if for some reason you want to find the eleventh item, we have only to visualise the tenth location quickly, and then we can move ahead to the eleventh. The same strategy can be used with linking – link a $5 bill between the fourth and sixth link.

IV. MEMORY TECHNIQUE OF THE STORY SYSTEM

In older times, story telling was a favourite pass-time. Our sages passed on their knowledge to their disciples who had to preserve it in their minds and later pass it on to others.

A close cousin to link system is the story system, in which each item in a list is linked to the one after it by an inter-connected story. The story system is different from the link method, in which each of the items is linked in an integrated narrative. This logical sequence may be easier for people to recall the analyst of simple but un-related paired associations. On the other hand, the story system can take more time, because we have to fit all the items into the story. The story system becomes progressively more difficult as the length of the list grows. It does not really matter how many items are there in the link method. In link method we can recall the item either backward or forward but in the story system it becomes difficult.

SCIENTIST'S VIEW ABOUT LINK AND STORY SYSTEM

Scientists, who have studied the link and story system, have found that both systems can help people learn and remember word lists. In fact, there is evidence that those who learn through the link system can remember up to three times as much as those who don't learn the techniques. Researches have also revealed that the story method is effective with abstract words and that un-related sentence can be remembered when they were strung together as a story.

Both methods have also been shown to be more effective than the use of imagery or rehearsal alone. When the order of the recall was important, the superiority of these mnemonic techniques was even greater.

V. MEMORY TECHNIQUE OF THE PEG SYSTEM

Peg systems are probably among the best known of all the memory systems. The use of peg words is a type of mnemonic strategy in which items to be remembered are mentally pegged to (associated with) certain images in a pre-arranged order. This method is superior to both the link and loci method because it is not dependent on sequential retrieval. We can access any item on the list without having to work our way through all the items before it.

There are a number of similarities between peg and loci methods. In both items to be remembered are associated with previously memorized concrete items, thus creating a sort of mental filing system. Peg words in the peg method and locations in loci method are used in the same fashion, and both peg words and locations can be used over and over again. Recall is also similar for both.

Thus peg system is a memory technique in which standard set of peg words (concrete nouns) are learned and items to be remembered are linked to the pegs with visual imagery. The system got its name from the fact that peg words act as mental pegs or hooks on which a person hangs the information that needs to be remembered. It is the most famous mnemonic devices, popular with entertainers and students of memory training. The pegs words help organise material that needs to be remembered and act as reminders to recall the material. A number of studies have shown that people are able to use the peg system effectively on lists up to 40 words long. It can also be used for remembering ideas, and similar applications.

There are a number of different peg systems, all of which use a concrete object to represents each number. The difference lies in the various ways to choose the objects that represent each number. The system includes the rhyme method, the look-alike method (shape method), Phonetic peg method and the value method. Most peg systems do not include a peg word for 0. The rhyme method uses Hero for Zero and value method uses Zero as empty box, phonetic peg uses 'Sea for zero' and look-alike method uses Zero as Bangles etc.

A. RHYME PEGS METHOD:

The best examples of rhymes ever known are the Vedas. Vedas consists of four parts.

1. Samhitas
2. Brahmanas
3. Aranyakas
4. Upanishads

Vedic hymns have typical rhythm. Even though Vedas originated long ago, they passed down the generations orally.

Because of their typical rhyme pattern and melody, Vedic hymns have been easily remembered and passed down for generations. Instead of trying to remember isolated words, first put them into specific rhymes and repeat them a few times. Now it is easy to remember them irrespective of the meaningfulness of the new sentence or verse thus formed. The reason for this is the rhythm.

The subject you have to study may be dry and boring. You may take out some important words from the lesson with that particular rhythm. Repeat the rhythm a number of times. That's all. You can recall the contents of the lesson by remembering the rhythm. If you find some problem in remembering the words of the rhythm you have composed, don't worry. Just chant the rhythm by stuffing it with gibberish. Repeat it one or two times. Try to remember at least one or two actual word replacement for gibberish words. Then you automatically remember the whole lesson. By practice you can master this art.

The rhymes method involves in every English alphabet sound and converts into similar words. See the examples below:

A	:	Ape	N	:	Hen
B	:	Bee	O	:	Hole
C	:	Sea	P	:	Pea
D	:	Dean	Q	:	Queen
E	:	Eel	R	:	Hour
F	:	Half	S	:	Snake
G	:	Jean	T	:	Tea
H	:	Itch	U	:	Universe
I	:	Eye	V	:	Wheel
J	:	Jay	W	:	Trouble
K	:	Cake	X	:	Eggs
L	:	Hell	Y	:	Wine
M	:	Ham	Z	:	Zip

Rhyming Jingles: This is a technique suitable for literature students and also for students who are willing to experiment in academics. A classic example is the nursery rhyme:

Thirty days have September,
April, June and November,
The entire rest has thirty-one
Except February alone.

The technique can be suitably altered to remember those confusing history dates.

EXAMPLES:

Discovery of America in 1942.
Columbus sailed the ocean blue
In fourteen hundred and ninety two.

Fire of London in 1966.
In sixteen hundred and sixty six,
London was burnt like rotten stick

This is the fast, simplest and effective method of generating mental image. It will help us in generating the first twenty memory codes. In this method we shall take the help of pronunciation of the number to decide its mental image/code.

Let's start with the number one. One is similar in pronunciation to the word sun or nun or bun etc. Now we need to select any one of them. Let's select sun. So from now onwards our mental image for one is sun.

Similarly think something that rhymes with two. It is essential to make the memory image as imaginative, as colourful and as bright as possible. For example for the number 2 we can visualise something similar in pronunciation like zoo or shoe. Our mental image for 3 can be tree or knee.

Let's select one mental memory code each for first 20 numbers.

One	Sun
Two	Shoe/Zoo
Three	Tree
Four	Door
Five	Wife/Knife
Six	Vicks
Seven	Heaven
Eight	Plate/Slate
Nine	Wine
Ten	Hen/Den
Eleven	Lemon
Twelve	Shelve
Thirteen	Thirsting (visualise a thirsty Man with a glass of water)
Fourteen	Fort in (entering into a big fort)
Fifteen	Lifting (weight lifter)
Sixteen	Sweet sixteen (a beautiful girl)
Seventeen	Seth in (a fat seth)
Eighteen	Attacking (scene of a war)
Nineteen	Namkeen
Twenty	Aunty (your favourite aunty)

Take the problem of the shopping list. If you wait until just before you leave the house to shop to write down what you need, you know what usually happens.

The use of the mental filing system instead of a written shopping list is the solution to your troubles You make upyour list as you go along, and retain it in your head.

For the sake of practice let us take a fairly typical shopping list and see how the items may be fitted reliably on the twenty memory codes, we already know:

1. Shirt 2. Ball 3. Calculator   4. Knife 5. Cake 6. Pepsi 7. Football 8. Soap 9. DDT 10. Stapler 11. Watch 12. Tiffin box13. Potato 14. Rubber 15. Mirror

Let's try to memorize the items with the help of memory codes.

1. Sun with shirt: Visualise your wet shirt is drying in the sunlight.

2. Ball with shoe: You are unable to wear a shoe since balls are inside

3. Calculator with tree: A tree on which a lot of calculators are hanging

4. Knife with door: Unable to open the door, so cutting with knife

5. Cake with wife: Offering cake to wife on her birthday

6. Pepsi with Vicks: Angry at the shopkeeper when you got the taste of Vicks from the Pepsi

7. Football with heaven: You hit the ball so hard that it went to heaven

8. Soap with plate:Applying soap on plate to clean it

9. DDT with wine: Dissolving DDT in wine to purify it

10. Stapler with hen: Stapling hen's beak so that it may not disturb you by cocking

11. Watch with lemon: After peeling off the lemon you got a watch inside

12. Tiffin box with shelf: A lot of Tiffin box scattered on the shelf and you are arranging them

13. Potato with thirsting: Eating potato dish and drinking lots of water

14. Rubber with fort in: Sweeper cleaning the wall of fort with rubber

15. Mirror with lifting: A weightlifter is lifting a heavy mirror

When you visualise according to the above-mentioned way, you have prepared a list of items, which you want to buy from market. Now you can easily recall the items serially and can buy all the items without missing anyone of them.

B. LOOK – ALIKE (SHAPE PEGS) METHOD:

We have memorized the memory codes from 1 to 20 with the help of rhyme method. For learning more codes we will take help of shape method. More codes mean more mental racks to store data in our memory.

We will create Shape Code FROM 1 TO 20 codes as follows:

1	Stick (One looks like a stick)
2	Duck (we can make a duck with digit 2)
3	Heart/Om (we can make a symbol of heart or Om by digit 3)
4	Chair (looks like a chair)
5	Hook (Looks like a hook)
6	Hockey stick (Looks like a hockey stick)
7	Lamp post (Looks like a lamp post)
8	Spectacles (We can make a shape of spectacle with 8)
9	Lolly pop (Looks like a lolly pop)

10   Bat and ball (Looks like a bat and ball)

11   Legs/wickets (Looks like two legs)

12   Door knob (We can make a picture of a door knob with 1 and 2)

13   Bow (We can make a bow by joining 1 and 3)

14   Flag (We can make a shape of a flag with 14)

15   Sitar (We can make a shape of sitar with1 and 5)

16   Elephant's trunk (We can make a shape of an elephant trunk by using 1 and 6)

17   Bread Pakauda (We can make a triangular bread pakauda by joining 1 & 7)

18   Binocular (We can make a shape of a binocular with digit1 and 8)

19   Nut Cracker (We can make a shape of a nut cracker by joining 1 and 9)

20   Scooter (We can make a shape of an old scooter by digit 2 and 0)

C. PHONETIC PEGS METHOD:

The great Harry Lorayne, who is credited with having a phenomenal memory, introduced a system, which if followed, also sharpens one's memory. It is called the peg system to remember numbers. Since the numbers are abstract and tangible, they have to be associated with something already we know, in order to remember them.

As it is well known, people in general find it difficult and have to struggle to recall telephone numbers, car numbers, pin codes, dates, events, anniversary, appointments etc. By using phonetic system, these figures can easily be remembered.

Phonetic means sound. Here, alphabet refers not just to English but also to any language in the world. In this method, we give different code to the numericals from 0 to 9.

Number	Corresponding Sounds	Reasons
1	T, D	Both alphabets sound alike and are written with one single down stroke. The letters have one down stroke.
2	N	Two down strokes in writing n.
3	M	Three down strokes in writing m.
4	R	FouR sound ends with 'R'.
5	L	Five fingers in the shape of "L", which is the Roman number for 50 also.
6	J, Ch, Sh	J is mirror image of 6. Ch sounds such church, chill, chase, cheese, cheque, march etc. Sh sounds such ship, shop, bush, and mush etc.
7	K, C, G	K involves two 7s. One 7 right side up, and the other upside down (K), C soft "C" pronounced as Cat, catch, coal etc. G pronounced as Ghee, god, and girl etc. All the above three sounds belong to one family.
8	F, V	If "f" continued, it would look like 8. Also when you pronounce fee, the sound V is also present. Written f and figure 8 both have two loops, one above the other (f -8)
9	P, B	P is the mirror image of No 9 and reverse position resembles alphabet 'B'. Both of them sound alike with diffent notation. The number 9 turned around P.
0	Z, S	When we pronounce zero, the sound of alphabet Z is involved, S is allotted for the reason that it resembles the sound shoonya (Zero in Hindi language); often Z and S are interchangeable in many words.

RULES FOR PHONETIC SYSTEM:

Pay attention only to the sound or pronunciation of word and not to the spelling. For example CAT: cat consists of two phonetic consonant. One is k and another is t. So we can make the code of 71 is CAT.

So here is the code from 1 to 100 based on phonetic peg system:

D. ALPHABET PEGS METHODS:

Numbers make a good peg system because they are naturally ordered and every one knows them. For this reason the alphabet makes a good peg system. Peg words can be created that rhyme with or sound similar to or the letters of the alphabet they represent or construct peg words without any rhymes using the letters of the alphabet to begin each word.

No	Code	No	Code	No	Code	No	Codess
1	Tea	26	Nisha (name)	51	Ludo	76	Catch
2	Knee	27	Neck	52	Lane	77	Cake
3	Ma	28	Nevea (cream)	53	Lame	78	Coffee
4	Ray	29	Nib	54	Lawyer	79	Cup
5	Hall	30	Maza	55	Lal (Mr Lal)	80	Fuse
6	Jaw	31	Mat	56	Lichi	81	Food
7	Key	32	Moon	57	Lake	82	Fan
8	Fee	33	Mama	58	Loaves	83	Foam
9	Bee	34	Mare	59	Lap	84	Fur
10	Dosa	35	Mail	60	Cheese	85	File
11	TTE	36	Mesh	61	Jet	86	Fish
12	Den	37	Mike	62	Chain	87	Fog
13	Dam	38	Movie	63	Jam	88	FIFA(World Cup)
14	Deer	39	Map	64	Jar	89	VIP
15	Doll	40	Rose	65	Jail	90	Bus
16	DJ	41	Rat	66	Chacha	91	Pet
17	Dock	42	Rain	67	Jug	92	Pen
18	TV	43	Rum	68	Chief	93	Balm
19	Tub	44	Rear	69	Jeep	94	Beer
20	Nose	45	Rail	70	Kiss	95	Bell
21	Net	46	Raja	71	Gate	96	Badge
22	Nun	47	Rock	72	Gun	97	Peak
23	Neem	48	Roof	73	Gum	98	Buffet ('T' is silent)
24	Neer(water)	49	Rope	74	Car	99	Papa
25	Nail	50	Lace('C'pronounced as 'S')	75	Kela (banana)	100	Dices

In Rhyme methods we made pegs of alphabets, here we make different pegs for alphabets. Creation of many pegs is helpful in memorising large numbers of information. More pegs means better memory. It is an addition to our mental racks. For example:

A	=	Apple	B	=	Ball	C	=	Cat
D	=	Dog	E	=	Elephant	F	=	Fish
G	=	Goat	H	=	Horse	I	=	Ink-pot

J	=	Jelly	K	=	Kangaroo
M	=	Mask	N	=	Needle
P	=	Parrot	Q	=	Queen
S	=	Snake	T	=	Tie
V	=	Violin	W	=	Window
Y	=	Yak	Z	=	Zebra

L = Lamp
O = Owl
R = Rat
U = Umbrella
X = X-ray

E. VALUE PEG'S METHOD:

No	Code	No	Code	No	Code
1	King	6	Sixes of Sachin	11	Team of football
2	Couple	7	Rainbow colour	12	Dozen
3	Three monkey of Gandhijee	8	Octopus	13	Unlucky man (Picturise a horrible person or a scene)
4	Four wheelers	9	Nine Planets	14	14 years exile of Lord Rama
5	Five Pandavas	10	Heads of Ravan	15	Independence day (15th August)

VI. MEMORY TECHNIQUE OF PERSONALISED MEANING SYSTEM (PMS)

The personalized meaning of word is based on the pronunciation of that particular word and related image in personal memory. For example:

Australia: PMS for Australia can be (in mind language) An Ash Tray, or A kangaroo or any individual favourite player of Australia team. Or break the word as ASH – TRAY, visualise Aishwariya Rai applying ash from a tray on her face for improving her colour.

Germany: PMS for Germany can be the mental picture of MANY GERMS or THE FACE OF CHANCELLOR OF GERMANY.

Magnesium: PMS for this can be a MAGNATE or A MUG ON WHICH MAP OF ASIA IS PAINTED.

Netherland: Try to observe the word Netherland and bifurcate the word to get a new meaning:Net – Her – Land. Now visualise a lady (Her) with a big Net covering a Land.

Cayman Island: KEY – MAN. Visualise a man with a big key is trying to open his house.

Israel: IS – REAL. Visualise that everything is real in that country.

Japan: PAN. Visualise a person named Japesh eating Pan.

South Korea: SEAT – CAR. Visualise an important person sitting on the seat of a car and driving.

Mauritius: MAUR – SHOES. Visualise a 'More' (Peacock in Hindi) wearing big shoes and dancing.

Mathematical signs: Every mathematical sign can be given a suitable meaning so that it can be handy while constructing a formula and any other symbolic terms. We may create a PMS for mathematical sign as follow:

+ Church	O Hole	– Hynes
△ Pyramid	X Fence	

PMS FOR ELEMENTS:

Name Of Elements	PMS
1. Carbon	Car full of bun
2. Hydrogen	High Dragon
3. Beryllium	Bury Him
4. Nitrogen	Night o' gin
5. Oxygen	Ox – gin
6. Fluorine	Floor – Urine
7. Phosphorous	Prosperous
8. Titanium	Titan – Him

9. Selenium   Sell U & Him
10. Praseodymium   Praise the Minimum
11. Bismuth   Big Mouth
12. Gadolinium   God only
13. Armstrong   Arm – Strong
14. Hysteresis   His Sisters

PMS OF PLACES:

TOWN		PMS
Haridwar	-	Hari ka Dwar
Kanpur	-	Pura Kan (The whole ear)
Jallandhar	-	Jal Ke andar (in the water)
Amritsar	-	Amrit ka sar (Head of Amrit) or Golden temple
Delhi	-	Dil le lia (you have stolen heart) or Red Fort
Bhatinda	-	Bhara hua tinda (Stuffed vegetable)
Chandigarh	-	Chandi devi ka Ghar (Home of Chandi)
Karnataka	-	Natak kar (Do a play)
Gujrat	-	Gujri huee raat (Night that have passed)
Surat	-	Face

With above examples you can make any PMS for anything, which you want to memorize. The main purpose of PMS is to create a linked mental picture, which is easily stored in our subconscious memory bank.

VII. MEMORY TECHNIQUE OF MIND MAPPING

Students face difficulty in assembling their thoughts after going through verbose class notes. And when the exams knock at the door, they end up sticking to guidebooks. Most of us, in our daily lives, face the same problem of taking a decision or finding a solution.

. Having identified this, two British scholars – Tony Buzan, world's leading author and lecturer on the brain and his brother Bary Buzan, a professor at the London school of Economics, penned "The Mind Map Book," a ground breaking, colourful note-making techniques which propounded the idea of "Radiant Thinking" and its best natural expression: mind mapping. Mind maps, also termed as "The Swiss army knife for the brain".

The colourful mind maps, where we see more of the pictures in colours leave indelible mark on the network of tunnels (suggested by the guru of lateral thinking Edward De Bono) in your brain. And the results are incredible, because colours and pictures are one of the memory languages of the mind.

People from all walks of life, for Example, Leonardo da Vinci, Isaac Newton, Albert Einstein, Thomas Edison, Beethoven, James Joyce, Vincent van Gogh, Mark twain – all used mind mapping to express themselves in a way that reflects the full range of their mental skills.

The standard linear note taking style of students at all levels in school, college and university only allows part of the complete picture to us as there is no free radiation of ideas. These notes lack the visual rhythm and pattern, colour, image, visualisation, association, dimension, spatial awareness etc, hence nothing new emerges. This technique utilizes only a fraction of the brain's enormous learning potential.

Mind mapping is the concept of radiant thinking that brings the gigantic data resting in our brain cells to its logical conclusion, where we start learning in a better and faster way.

Radiant thinking refers to the associative thought processes that proceed from or connect to a central point, leading to a coloured graphic image called mind map. It provides a universal key to unlocking the potential of the brain. The mind map harnesses the full range of cortical skills- words, image, number, logic, rhythm, colour and spatial awareness- in a single, uniquely powerful technique.

HOW TO START MIND MAPPING:

In the beginning, the mind mapper creates a central theme from which, associations spread in the form of branches and sub-branches and so on. Every key word or image thus added itself, which brings the possibility of a new and greater range of associations. More and more related and unrelated ideas occur during the process, forming patterns of association.

In order to create a mind map we first identify our Basic Ordering Ideas (BOIs) that are key concepts within which a host of other concepts can be organised. For example, the term 'machines' contains a vast array of categories, one of which is 'motor vehicles'. This in turn, generates a large range, one of which is 'cars'. This brings in the type of car such as Maruti that can again be subdivided into various models. So machines would be BOI not Maruti as 'machines'.

If mind mappers give more emphasis to colours, pictures, codes, dimensions, diagrams, numbers etc. their mind maps become more interesting and entertaining which, in turn, aid creativity, enhance memory and specially the recall of information.

The full power of the mind map is realized by having a central image instead of a central word, and by using images wherever appropriate rather than words. The capacity of recognition memory for picture is almost limitless. Pictures are evocative than words, more precise and potent in triggering a wide range of associations, thereby enhancing creative thinking and memory.

MIND MAP LAWS:

Use emphasis on the following:

- Always use a central image.
- Use images throughout your mind map.
- Use more colours per central image.
- Use dimension in images and around words.
- Use kinesthesia (the blending of the physical senses)
- Use variations of size of printing, line and image.
- Use organised spacing.
- Use appropriate spacing.
- Use association:
- Use arrows when you make connections within and across the branch pattern.
- Use colours.
- Use codes.

Be clear:

- Use only one key per line
- Use capital letters for all words.
- Use capital key words on lines.
- Make the line length equal to word length.

The three 'As' of mind mapping are:

1. Accept: Accept means one should set aside any preconceptions one may have about one's mental limitations and follow the mental mapping laws and recommendations correctly.

2. Apply: It is the second stage for developing our own mind mapping style.

3. Adapt: It refers to the ongoing development of the mind mapping skills.

Thus, after following the mind mapping laws, one can reach a stage where things become immensely clear. With the help of well-crafted mind map, we can organise ours as well as other peoples' ideas; enhance memory; think creatively; create a group mind by bringing individuals together; analyze yourself; solve personal problems; maintain a mind map diary; presentations; management; teaching; story-telling, etc. the choice is enormous.

VIII. MEMORY TECHNIQUE OF MENTAL FILING SYSTEM

It is a system designed to organise and stack our ideas, facts and figures in an orderly manner in the storehouse of our memory bank and facilitate easy recall to the showroom of our conscious mind whenever we need them. Effective usage of this system enables us to store any amount of information, facts, figures and sections of legal acts etc.

The human brain has no match in sorting out, storing and recalling information. It can beat the best computer in the world because it is much faster and more flexible than any man-made device. But still we do not rely on our natural memory system and retain diaries, index books, notebooks, digital diaries and other memory aids.

In a good office, correspondence is filed properly. Information may be filed in various ways depending on the nature of work, but the most common criterion is subject. Files on similar subject may be opened under a common heading or sub heading and accordingly filed in a given drawer or cabinet. Good filing is essential for fast and efficient retrieval. If the numbers of files are large, they may be indexed. Old sites may be recorded and stored in a separate place, which may be away from the immediate work place.

In computer too, materials are saved in files. Files on the same subject are grouped together in separate directory or sub directory. This file may be retrieved easily, acted upon and again closed and stored.

In many respects, the mind works like a computer, It is, therefore, very necessary that after giving the mind an order to note something properly and memorize it, we must help the mind file it properly too. In most memory matters, quick retrieval is very essential. We need to recall the name of familiar person immediately on meeting him or her. We must keep on talking and recalling what we have to say next in a speaking assignment. So there is simply no scope to rummage around before coming up with the relevant file. We must have instant recall and for this, proper filing is essential.

Improper filing creates confusion. It is not enough to file similar facts together. Each separate fact must exist as distinctly as possible. Our brain is just like the hard disc of a computer. As we store various files in the hard disc, we can also store information in our brain and recall it at will. The key is to store the information in a systematic manner.

Creation of Mental Files: Mental files can be created as many as we want, we must associate and name the files after a person whom we know or any object, which we know around us. For examples we can name the even number file after male names we know and odd number files can be named after female names known to us. Names can be of our family members, relatives, friends, teachers, role models, sports person, actor, actress, god and goddesses etc. We can easily remember the numerical digits by mental filing system. When numbers are given to these persons or objects in the memory file and associated with the peg word, we will be able to recall the digits by using their association later. For example:

SL No.	Name of the file
1.	Mother's name
2.	Father's name
3.	Aunt's name
4.	Uncle's name
5.	Sister's name

6.   Brother's name
7.   Sister in law's name
8.   Brother in law's name
9.   Goddess Laxmi
10.   God Narayana & so on.

Suppose you want to memorize the properties of electron. Give name to electron as No 1 file. Associate it with another. And assign the properties of electron in animated form by associating with your mother. Thus file is ready. Whenever you want to recall about electron just visualise the mother and recollect the things from your memory. These mental files can be extra tools apart from other mental pegs to memorize anything.

IX. MEMORY TECHNIQUE OF COMPREHENSION METHOD

It is the method of remembering by understanding. This procedure works well for science subjects, where understanding of the procedure or the process becomes very important. Try to comprehend the subject under six headings that is why, where, what, when, who and how. Hence after reading the matter once, try to understand what you have read by asking these questions. It is a permanent way of remembering.

Regarding your studies ask the following questions:

- What are my problems regarding studies?

- When should I start preparing for my examinations?

- Why am I tensed about studies and examinations?

- How can I overcome my tension and stress regarding studies?

- From where should I start studying?

- Whose help should I take or whom should I consult regarding my studies?

Change your study method: When you read for 4 to 5 hours everyday, you should read for one hour and take a break of ten minutes. The question is what you need to do during this ten minute break?

As we know, "comprehending and recalling" are very important parts of memory, so we need to practice the same. After reading for an hour, sit in another chair, close your eyes and try to recall what you have read for the last one hour. Initially, you will be shocked to see that you can hardly recall anything. After 10 minutes of this exercise, go back for reading once again. This will reinforce the learning and understanding. When you read for five hours you will recall for (5 multiplied by 10 minutes) 50 minutes. This will enhance your understanding and recalling ability. Hence, there will be no question of you missing any information in the examination hall.

X. MEMORY TECHNIQUE OF MECHANICAL METHOD

The mechanical method of remembering is also called the 'by heart' method or rote Method of remembering. This method can be effectively used to remembering definitions, equations, formulae, names, multiplication tables etc. This method should not be used for remembering procedures or processes.

Many students and adults use this method in their day to day life. As repetition is the mother of memory, it will definitely help us to remember a lot of things. That is how a small child, by continuous repetition, can very easily recite many rhymes. The child does not even know the meaning of "twinkle, twinkle, little star, how I wonder what you are....." But he or she can still recite the poem.

Similarly, priests in temples or in churches can narrate number of 'shlokas' or verses because they have been doing it repeatedly. Even students can do the same. The only problem is that with many subjects and many chapters to be memorized in a short span of time, students have a lot on their plate.

To make this method work, after every hour of study, students need to recall and recap that they have learnt to see how much they can actually reproduce in an examination. If anything is missing it needs to be strengthened by a second reading. This method is much better than trying to cram huge masses of information at one go without checking how much of it has really sunk in.

If you need help in remembering facts and figures, first write down everything on a chart and paste it on a wall above your study or worktable. Read, observe and revise these for 10 minutes twice a day – preferably in the morning and at night. The results are almost instantaneous. Within a few days, these facts and figures will become so ingrained in your memory that you will never need to look at the chart again.

Hence, it is very important to know how we can do about the repetition process in a productive manner. The right procedure is to read today and repeat the same thing tomorrow. For example, spend 4 hours today to read chapter-I, tomorrow, when you repeat, you will require only 15 minutes to revise Chapter-I, the rest of the time can be spent on reading chapter-II. On third day, you need to spend only 5minutes on chapter-I, 15 minutes on chapter-II and rest of the time on chapter III. As you keep going, once in a fortnight, revise all the chapters. If you keep repeating this, all the chapters will be fresh in your mind on any given day.

To remember formulae, wherever you think you may go wrong, write these formulae in different Colour. They stay in our sub conscious mind for a long time. Red colour is more preferable as it has the longest wavelength and so it stands out more in comparison to the other colours.

20

REGISTRATION EXERCISES BASED ON MEMORY TECHNIQUES

To memorise the below data, you can create the mental image of Australia as A ASH TRAY TIED WITH LACE (CODE OF 50), MANY GERMS (as PMS for Germany) ON A RACK (CODE OF 47), AND GEORGE BUSH (as PMS for America) ADVERTIZING MINT (CODE OF 321 by PHONETIC SYSTEM).

A. MEMORISING NUMERICAL FIGURES:

Memorise the following:

NAME OF COUNTRIES	AMT. OF EXPORT (in million)
Australia	50000
Germany	47000
America	321000

B. MEMORISING PERIODIC TABLE OF CHEMISTRY

We can memorise the position of various elements in the periodic table by simple rule of acronym.

Let's try to learn the period II of the periodic table. Elements of the IInd period of the periodic table are as follow:

	ELEMENTS	SYMBOL	ATOMIC NO.
1	Lithium	Li	3
2	Beryllium	Be	4
3	Boron	B	5
4	Carbon	C	6

5	Nitrogen	N	7
6	oxygen	O	8
7	Fluorine	F	9
8	Neon	Ne	10

Let's make a sentence containing the entire symbol in the same order.

Lilly berry born Capricorn naturally studied at oxford than at flora nagar

Now the initial alphabets of the word will give the clue of the elements and also we can get the atomic number from the sentence since all the sequence of elements is maintained in it

PERIOD III OF THE PERIODIC TABLE

1	Sodium	Na	11
2	Magnesium	Mg	12
3	Aluminum	Al	13
4	Silicon	Si	14
5	Phosphorus	P	15
6	Sulphur	S	16
7	Chlorine	Cl	17
8	Argon	Ar	18

MEMORY SENTENCE FOR PERIOD III

Soda (Na) from Mango Tree (Mg) eliminates (al) silky (si) and fussy (p) sulphur (s) and clears (cl) arguments (ar)

Since the period IV is quite lengthy so it would be simpler to divide the period in 2 or 3 parts and make two or three sentence for each.

FOR INSTANCE FOR FIRST FIVE ELEMENTS OF PERIOD IV

1.	Potassium	K	19
2	Calcium	Ca	20
3	Scandium	Sc	21

| 4 | Titanium | Ti | 22 |
| 5 | Vanadium | V | 23 |

Memory sentence could be

Potato (K) from Calcutta (Ca) are sent (Sc) by Trucks (Ti) and Vans (V)

Similarly try to form memory sentence for other elements of different period.

Memorising the elements of Groups

ELEMENTS IN EACH GROUP ARE

Here group no is represented by value system of number pegs and personalised words (PMS) for elements as shown against them in next column.

GROUP 1		RAJA
Lithium	Li	Lichee
Sodium	Na	Soda-bottle
Potassium	K	Pot
Rubidium	Rb	Rubi Bhatia (T.V Anchor)
Cesium	Cs	Scissors
Francium	Fr	Frock

To remember group 1 elements you should link all the elements with Raja.

Association: Visualise that a Raja is eating lichee (Li) and drinking Soda (Na) by pouring it into a beautiful pot (K). He is also enjoying dance of Rubi Bhatia (Rb) who is wearing scissor (Cs) printing Frock (Fr).

GROUP 2		COUPLE
Beryllium	Be	Borolene
Magnesium	Mg	Maggie
Calcium	Ca	Calciumsandose tablets
Strontium	Sr	Strong

| Barium | Ba | Bar |
| Radium | Ra | Radio |

Association: Visualise a couple is holding borolene (Be). As they squeeze it, Maggie (Mg) comes out instead of cream. They are eating Maggie with small white calcium sandose tablets (Ca). They are getting strong (Sr) (See the muscles growing) as they eat it. Then they go to a bar (Ba) where they begin to dance to the music of radio (Ra).

GROUP 3		**THREE MONKEYS**
Scandium	Sc	Scan
Yttrium	Y	Stone – bow
Lanthanum	La	Lanka
Actinium	Ac	AC (Air Conditioner)

Association: For the second element Yttrium you should visualise the symbol Y as stone – bow. Next two elements have been personalized by giving a new word Lanka to Lanthanum and by considering Actinium as AC). So imagine that three monkeys are scanning (Sc), with a stone bow – Y to see if Sri Lanka has any A.C.

GROUP 4		**FOUR WHEELER**
Titanium	Ti	Titanic
Zirconium	Zr	Jerk
Hafnium	Hf	High
Rutherfordium	Rf	Roof

Association: Visualise a big Titanic ship (Ti) which is not propelling. So you have fitted wheels under it. Oh, what is this? It jerks (Zr). Being afraid you climb on the high (Hf) roof (Rf) of Titanic ship.

GROUP 5		**PANDAVAS**
Vanadium	V	Van
Niobium	Nb	Nib

Tantalum	Ta	Tent

Association: See in your mind that five pandavas are going on a van (V). they are shooting nibs (Ni). Nibs are striking altogether and make a big tent(Ta).

GROUP 6		**SIXER OF SACHIN**
Chromium	Cr	Crow
Molybdenum	Mo	Mobile
Tungsten	W	Tongue

Association: Sachin Tendulkar is playing cricket. He hits sixes. See the ball going up in the sky. Oh, the ball hits a crow (Cr) who is talking on a mobile (Mb). As the ball hit, the crow sticks out its tongue (W).

GROUP 7		**RAINBOWS**
Maganese	Mn	Mango
Technetium	Tc	Technician

Association: On a rainbow, mangoes (Mn) are being fitted to make it more beautiful by a technician (Tc).

GROUP 8		**OCTOPUSES**
Iron	Fe	Iron
Ruthenium	Ru	Rath (Chariot)
Osmium	Os	Philosopher

Association: Visualise an octopus is driving an iron (Fe) made rath (Ru). In the rath Osho (Os) is sitting.

GROUP 9		**NINE PLANETS**
Cobalt	Co	Bolt
Rhodium	Rh	Road
Iridium	Ir	Indian

Association: In order to connect planets you are using bolt (Co, see big bolts) and making a road (Rh) for Indians (Ir) only.

GROUP 10

Nickel	Ni
Palladium	Pd
Platinum	Pt

RAVAN WITH TEN HEADS

Knickers
Paddle
Plate

Association: Ravan is wearing knickers (Ni) and paddling (Pd) a boat which is made out of plates (Pt)

GROUP 11

Copper	Cu
Silver	Ag
Gold	Au

Football team

Cup
Silver
Gold

Association – Football players have won silver (Ag) and gold (Au) cups (Cu) in the prize.

GROUP 12

Zinc	Zn
Cadmium	Cd
Mercury	Hg

ONE DOZEN BANANA

Zin (Helpful spirit)
Candle
Mercury

Association: You have got one dozen bananas. As you peel a banana a zin (Zn) comes out with a burning candle (Cd) which is made of mercury (Hg).

GROUP 13

Boron	B
Aluminium	Al
Gallium	Ga
Indium	In
Thallium	Ti

HORRIBLE

Bora (Sack)
Aluminium Rod
Gali (Street)
Indian
Thali (Big Plate)

Association: you have seen some horrible event so you are scared and enter a Bora (B) to hide yourself but what do you see there? There are so many aluminium rods (Al). As you enter, one of the aluminium rods you find it long gali (Ga) in which on both the sides Indian (In) people are standing holding big thalis (Ti).

GROUP 14		RAM'S EXILE FOR 14 YEAR
Carbon	C	Car
Silicon	Si	Sali (Sister in law)
Germanium	Ge	Germany
Tin	Sn	Tin
Lead	Pb	Lead pencil

Association: Visualise Ram is going for 14 yrs exile in a car (C) along with his Sali (Si) to Germany (Ge) and people are giving them a tin (Sn) full of lead pencils (Pb).

GROUP 15		15TH AUGUST
Nitrogen	N	Night
Phosphorus	P	Fox with pores
Arsenic	As	Sainik (Soldiers)
Antimony	Sb	Aunty
Bismuth	Bi	Biscuit

Association: On 15th August, at night (N) foxes (P) are doing Independence Day parade wearing sainik (As) uniforms and an aunty (Sb) is distributing biscuits (Bi) among them.

GROUP 16		SWEETS
Oxygen	O	Ox
Sulphur	S	Fur
Selenium	Se	Saloon
Tellurium	Te	Talcum powder
Polonium	Po	Polo

Association: Visualise an Ox (O) eating a lot of sweets (16) and suddenly fur (S) grows on his body. He goes to a Saloon (Se) to get them removed. The saloon man puts talcum powder (Te) and gives him Polo (Po) as medicine.

GROUP 17		7'UP TIN
Fluorine	F	Floor
Chlorine	Cl	Clown
Bromine	Br	Broom
Iodine	I	Iodex
Astatine	At	Ass

Association: See lots of 7'up tins lying on floor (F). a clown (Cl) comes and cleans it with the Broom (Br) and applies Iodex (I) on the floor. Suddenly an ass (At) comes and spoils it again.

GROUP 18		VOTERS AGE
Helium	He	Helen (Old actress)
Neon	Ne	Peon
Argon	Ar	Gun
Krypton	Kr	Cry
Xenon	Xe	Zeenat Aman (Actress)

Association: In an election campaign Helen (He) is dancing and a peon (Ne) with a gun (Ar) is standing besides, for her protection but peon cries (Kr) as Zeenat Aman (Xe) comes to kill Helen.

MEMORISING ELEMENTS AND THEIR ATOMIC NO

I. Hydrogen : (Sun – Hydrogen Balloon)
    Imagine a big and beautiful hydrogen balloon going up in the sky towards the sun

ii. Helium : (Shoe – Helen)
    Imagine Helen is dancing, wearing shoe around her neck.

iii. Lithium : (Tree – Lichee)
    Imagine you are plucking red tasty lichees from tree.

iv. Beryllium : (Door – Borolene)

Imagine you are applying borolene on the door of your room.

v. Boron : (Knife – Bora)
Imagine you are cutting a 'bora'(Jute bag) with a knife

vi. Carbon : (Vicks – Car)
Imagine you are rubbing Vicks on your brand new car to make it shiny.

vii. Nitrogen : (Heaven – Night)
Imagine at night you see dreams of heaven.

viii. Oxygen : (Plate – ox)
Imagine you are feeding an ox from a big plate.

ix. Fluorine : (Wine – Floor)
Imagine today you are washing your floor with wine

x. Neon : (Hen – Peon)
Imagine on your school gate, a hen is sitting in the place of peon.

Rest of the elements can be memorised by following the same method of visualisation.

C. MEMORISING HISTORICAL DATA

We can use our memory system to memorise historical data. Example: Suppose we have to learn the following incidents

1. 1921 – Gandhiji assumed leadership of the congress party

We know that the code of 21 is net by phonetic method. Therefore we will form mental picture as:

Mental picture: When Gandhiji was giving speech as he was elected leader, Englishmen captured him by throwing the net on him.

2.   1933 - Hitler became Chancellor of Germany
        Code for 33 is Mama

Mental picture: Hitler is gifting a pack of big chancellor cigarette to your mama on becoming chancellor of his country.

3.   1927 – Television demonstrated for the first time
        Code for 27 is Neck

Mental picture: A big crowd is watching TV which is hanging around the neck of a tall person.

Here in all the three cases we have not included the century year that is 19. Since we know that we will not confuse them with any other century.

You can use this system to memorise other historical events also.

4.   1452 – 1519 William Shakespeare, English playwright.
        To remember the dates, convert these years into peg
        words-Door, Lion & doll, Deep

Mental Picture: Visualise Shakespeare being born and a lion standing at the door. He died when the doll went deep into the ground.

Now we can memorise any historical dates on the basis of above examples.

D. MEMORISING BIOLOGICAL TERMS

For Example:

1.   Vitamin A (Retinol): Deficiency of Vitamin 'A' causes
        night blindness.

To memorise above you can create a picture of A RAT STUCK UP IN A NAL (WATER PIPE) AND UNABLE TO SEE DUE TO DARKNESS IN THE PIPE.

2.   Vitamin D (Cholecalciferol): Deficiency causes Rickets

To memorise this you can visualise COAL FROM CALCUTTA IS FERRIED IN A DOUBLE DECKER (PMS FOR CHOLECALCIFEROL) WHICH WAS DESTROYED BY A ROCKET (PMS FOR RICKETS) FIRED ON THE WAY.
You can create your own mental picture depending on your creativity for purpose of retaining in memory comfortably and creating an environment for learning with fun.

E. MEMORISING VOCABULARY

The best way to remember word meaning is to find a linking word and create a PMS for association. For Example:

WORD	MEANING	LINKING WORD
1 ABLUTION	WASHING	LOTION

You can create a mental picture of washing a blue (pms for ablution is blue lotion) uniform with lotion.

2 EXCULPATE	TO CLEAR FROM BLAME	EX CULPRIT

You can create a mental picture of a culprit is being acquitted by a court and now he is an ex culprit.

3 HEGEMONY	SUPERIORITY	HEDGE

You can create a mental picture of your superior hiding money in a hedge (long bushes)

F. MEMORISING SPELLINGS

i. By Highlighting the letters: For Example:

SEPERATE: This is wrong spelling. Correct spelling is SEPARATE. Now write separate as sep-A-rate five times highlighting A in a different colour so that it can be automatically registered in memory (because colour is a mind language)

ii. By correcting the errors: For Example:

a. ACOMODATE : This is wrong spelling. Correct it and write it as follows in different colour shades.

accoMModate

b. EMBARASS: this is wrong spelling. Correct it and write it as follows:

embaRRass

Visualisation is the key to remember the correct spelling. As far as possible try to create a mental picture by colouring and shading the mistakes.

G. REMEMBERING NAMES AND FACES

Faces are easier to remember than the names. Because the images of faces is a mind language and name is not a mind language. Therefore apply following rules to memorise names and faces:

1. OBSERVE THE FACE
2. LOOK FOR OUTSTANDING FEATURES (ANY MARK, CUT, HAIR STYLE, NOSE SHAPE, EARS SHAPE, NECK, HANDS, FINGERS ETC.)

3. MENTALLY DRAW THE FACE WITH OUTSTANDING FEATURES OBSERVED.

4. GET THE NAME CLEARLY AND REPEAT THE NAME IMMEDIATELY AFTER THE INTRODUCTION

5. SEE WHETHER THE NAMES HAS MEANING IN ITSELF AND EASIER TO PICTURISE

6. CONNECT THE NAME WITH FACE WITH FUNNY ASSOCIATION AND IMAGINE IT.

7. YOU CAN ASSOCIATE THE NEW FACES WITH OLD KNOWN NAMES   AND FACES

H. MEMORISING IMPORTANT ORES, REAGENTS AND CHEMICALS

To remember ores, reagents and chemicals we shall link these common names with their corresponding chemical formulae.

i. Carnalite – KCl MgCl2 6H2O

If you try to memorise the formula of carnalite blindly, you may easily get confused in the formula and may even forget it. In order to give it a space in the permanent memory, we will make a conscious association between the name and the formula like this:

Substitution form by creating PMS

Carnalite	Car-light
KCl	Pot – clown
MgCl2	Maggie – clown (2)
6	Jaw (By phonetic)
H2O	Water

The substituted form of the formula will be:
Car-light = Pot-clown Maggie clown (2) jaw water

Now associate the entire substitute in a way that will remind us of the actual formula.

Mental Picture: Visualise that infront of a car-light, a clown is sitting holding pot containing Maggie. Meanwhile2 clowns come and fill his jaw with water.

Here is how you can remember even chemical equations this way:

CO_2	=	cone
N_2	=	Nun
CO_3	=	Comb
O_2	=	Own
$CuSO_4$=		Kishore

I. MEMORISING MAPS

The method for memorising the map is called GRID METHOD. The following steps should bear in mind while memorising maps:

i. Make an outline, outside the map in a rectangular form.

ii. Now divide this rectangle in 10 parts. Then mark it 0 to 9 and join the lines. This should be done with very light pencil.

iii. See the code. Each square is having a phonetic code like

00	Sauce
01	Tie
02	Eno
03	Ma
04	Ray
05	Hall

iv. Also visualise each square, as a room representing above items.

v. Now ascertain the locations, associate them with the square code and visualise it. For example: Suppose Delhi (on the map of India) falls in the square-74, associate it with car (code of 74) and visualise that in Delhi every body flies in car.

J. MEMORISING LONG THEORY OR ANSWERS IN POINTS:

Roof top method is very helpful in memorising any long theory, long answer and answer in points. This is one of the most interesting and easy techniques of memory. It helps in longer retention and quick and exact recall as the student himself becomes the part and parcel of the answer. This is made possible through VISUALISATION.

The basic principle of the Roof Top method is that you have to visualise the surrounding (According to the answer) and place yourself on the roof of a building, which is situated in that surrounding. Secondly, you have to engage yourself in an active conversation with the participants/persons mentioned in the answer. This can be understood by the following example. In this way you will have a rock solid memory, for that answer.

Example: Suppose you are a Civics student and have to memorise the following answer of a chapter 'Rural Community Development'. The objectives of Rural Community Development are being achieved by the following:

i. Farmers are provided with high-yielding seeds, modern agricultural implements, fertilizers and healthy cattle.

ii. Irrigation facilities are improved by construction of canals, digging wells and installing pumps.

iii. Wastelands are made suitable for agriculture by using fertilizers. Tree plantation has also been launched to stop soil erosion.

iv. Cultivators are encouraged to grow and increase the output of vegetables and fruits.

v. Modern methods of farming are taught.

vi. Schools and adult education centers are opened.

vii. Health care centers and family welfare centers are set up.

viii. Villages are being electrified.

For memorising these points, you have to see yourself as a person, wearing the rural clothes and standing on the roof of a hut. Now see that on a normal rural day, people are going for their jobs and women and children are enjoying a sunny day.

1. According to the first point: Farmers are provided with high yielding seeds, modern agricultural implements, fertilizers and healthy cattle. Now see yourself talking to a farmer, asking about seeds, its quality and price. See that you are also talking about the old and new agricultural implements, tractors and cattle etc.

2. According to the second point: From the roof of the hut you can see the big canal that was recently dug in the village. See that you are fixing up the price of digging and installing pumps with a plumber. Similar process can be adopted for the remaining points. Say for example, you can see that near the hut, on which you are standing, there is a pole of streetlight and you are switching on the light. Old men are studying in the adult education centers and you are the person who is teaching them.

The basic thrust of this sort of visualisation is to enliven the very content in full spirit so that everything gets solidly stored in the mind. Suppose you want to remember a list of abstract ideas; say you need to give a speech or presentation. Translate the abstract ideas into visual images of tangible objects. If you need to make a point about profit, visualise a business graph. If you need to mention product distribution, picture a truck or train. If you need to talk about a change in management attitude, envision a manager upside – down. When you need to recall series of ideas, just recall the objects.

K. MEMORISING COUNTRY- CAPITAL AND CURRENCY

For memorising country name and its capital, associate country's name with capital's name. Example:

1.   The capital of Bulgaria is Sophia.

Now create the PMS and visualise the picture of PMS images and then link those pictures.

Bulgaria – Bull Gira (Fell down),
Sophia – sofa set

You can visualise that a bull gira on the sofa set.

2.   The capital of USA is Washington

      PMS for USA – use and
      For Washington – Washing

Now visualise that you have used many clothes and you are washing them.

3.   The capital of Fiji is Suva.

      PMS for Fiji can be Fauji or soldiers and
      For Suva – can be a big needle (Suva)

Now you can see that soldiers don't have rifles and they are fighting with big needles in their hands.

4.   The currency of Italy is Lira.

PMS for Italy can be idly (a south Indian dish) and
For Lira – Lada (Fought)

Now see that you fought with your sister to get more idly.

Likewise you can memorise others by association method.

L. MEMORISING RECIPROCALS

1. Reciprocal of 28 is 0.0357

    Here, ignore the zero, since it appears in all the
    reciprocals. Now convert 357 into a peg word. MLK –
    MILK. The peg word for 28 is Knife. Now associate
    knife and milk. You have got the reciprocal for 28.

2. The reciprocal of 9 is 0.111. You can remember them by
    associating bee (9) with DDT (.111).

3. The reciprocal of 11 is 0.0909. Associate Daddy (11)
    with Busy Bee (.909).

M. MEMORISING SQUARES, CUBE ROOTS AND CUBE

1. The square root of 10 is 3.162. Convert them into
    peg words and associate 'Dosa' (10) with Ma (3) and
    touch in (162).

2. The square root of 21 is 4.58. Convert them into peg
    words and associate net (21) with Ray (4) and Leaf
    (58).

3. The square root of 30 is 5.477. Convert them into
    peg words and associate Mouse (30) with Lawyer
    (54) and raw cake (477).

4. The cube root of 2 is 1.26. Convert them into peg
    words and associate Knee (2) with Tie (1) and Naach
    (26) or Nisha (any known girl of this name)

5. The cube root of 3 is 1.44. Convert them into peg words and associate ma (3) with Tie (1) and Rear (44).

6. The cube root of 9 is 2.08. Convert them into peg words and associate Bee (9) with Knee (2) and sofa (08) or Fee.

7. The cube root of 21 is 2.75. Convert them into peg words and associate Net (21) with knee (2) and Kela (75).

8. The cube root of 29 is 3.072. Convert them into peg words and associate Nib (29) with Ma (3) and Skin (072) or with Mouse (30) and Gun (72)

9. The cube of 12 is 1728. Associate Don (12) with Toffee and Knife (1728).

10. The cube of 16 is 4096. associate dish (16) with Rose Beach (4096)

11. The cube of 29 is 24389. Associate Nib (29) with Noorie Move up (24389).

21

RETENTION

Retention is the important part of long term memory. Therefore you have to pay attention on following points to make your retention longer and permanent.

I. Make Lasting impressions in memory by creating colourful and natural images on the screen of your conscious mind and visualising it by your third eye

Visualisation becomes a positive study technique when it is used to maximize positive feelings and reduce negative ones. You can learn to bring up good memories on demand, using visualisation of the past. You can also learn to use images of how you want things to be, using visualisation of the future. The positive feelings and the brain physiology that underlie them are the same for each.

Experts believe that the easiest method to improve one's memory is to create mental pictures or images of people or matters and visualise them by linking with one another.

Exercise for Visualisation: - Think of a room. Sit on a chair and close your eyes. Try to relax. Imagine that there is a door. Enter the room through it. Imagine that it is a cozy, beautiful room painted in a lovely colour and fully furnished. Imagine there are shelves and cabinets to store books and files, a computer and a sound system. Feel peaceful, calm and relaxed. Recall a day when you were very happy. Hear the sounds and smell the aromas. You feel happier. At this point, put your thumb and index finger of left hand together and say that whenever you will do so, you will be back in your memory palace, and will be perfectly calm and relaxed and will easily get any information you need. This will certainly help to recall any information that is stored in this relaxed state.

II. Make an Effective Revision Plan

Revision is very necessary for Retention of something one has memorised. Without revision, one can not retain the required things for a long time.

Suppose you have memorised something. Now the question arises when should one revise for retaining it in the memory?

The first revision should be done within twenty four hours. On an average, one's brain is able to retain any fresh information up to 80-100 % only for 24 hours. After that it goes down and gets linked with already existing information that one has. The forgetting cycle speeds up by the end of 24 hrs. So the first revision must be completed within 24hrs of learning.

Once the fresh information is revised after 24hrs, the brain has the capacity to hold it for approximately next seven days. After that one must revise the topic for a second time so that it is permanently memorised for a long time. Follow this procedure for a month.

After a month you can revise it fortnightly and then monthly.

If you follow these time periods, your revision time will be only 10% of your total time. You will require only twelve minutes revising the entire topic because you do not need any note books to revise it. Your memory bank is the moving note book for you. Revision also keeps you away from opening of waste and negative files.

III. USE BOTH SIDES OF YOUR BRAIN

Medical science says that the left side of the brain deals with logic, language, numbers and sequence, while the right side is connected with visualisation of images, Colour and awareness. However, both hemispheres of the brain can undertake all kinds of activities. You should never say that you do not have the capacity to imagine or that you are weak in a certain subject. In fact, the logical answer is that you have not developed an interest in that particular subject. All you have to do is improve your memory in order to use both sides of the brain.

As you get older, you lose your imaginative skills. In other words, you use less of your right brain hemisphere. Take the case of children studying in lower classes. They cram classroom walls with Coloured drawings. They have boxes full of Coloured pencils, paints etc. When they reach higher classes, they are on the move, from one room to another and visual stimulation is absent. Most of them stop learning in the new environment.

The lesson to be learnt here is that if we want a powerful memory, we have to retain material in the brain so effectively that we can recall it after an hour or even after a year.

HOW TO USE BOTH PARTS OF BRAIN

The human brain is a paired organ; it is composed of two halves, called cerebral hemisphere. The theory of the structure and functions of the brain suggests that the two sides of the brain related to two different modes of thinking.

Just stop to wonder for a moment how a two - year old baby can master the task of speaking so effortlessly while most adult efforts at learning a foreign language tend to end up as more effort and less learning? Most children are born with right hemisphere dominant, when an infant learns a language, she does so with all her senses of smell, sounds, colours, feelings etc. As we grow older, the left hemisphere modes of thinking which rely heavily on partial processes (without visualisations) of the intellect (logic, sequence, organisation) become dominant.

In the Zen tradition the left mind is associated with the process of thinking and the right mind is associated with knowing. Most individuals tend to have a distinct preference for one or the other side of the brain. From very early in life, school and society too conspire to identify individual as one or the other (Arts or the Science) and label them as "Creative or logical"

USING THE OTHER HAND

It has been established that the right brain, which is connected with a person's intuitive, creative and holistic faculties, is linked to left hand movements, while the left brain whose functions are logical, analytical and rational, is linked to right hand movements. Thanks to the over emphasis on the written word and paperwork, all of which are left brain activities done with the right hand. The chances are that schooling has left you with a lopsided brain development. Such acts like brushing our teeth or combing our hair with the non-dominant hand (in the most cases the left) if incorporated into our routine can help stimulate the creative brain.

DO FAMILIAR TASKS DIFFERENTLY

Try showering or starting the car with your eyes shut or read a page or two upside down, or simply shut the eyes for a few minutes and explore the room with the other senses – touch, smell, background noises etc. to tune into the right brain. These simple acts force you out of the most frequently utilized areas of your mind and into areas less utilized.

PICTURE THE PROBLEM

Stuck on the problem and with nowhere to go? Try depicting it pictorially – yes, drawing it out, using colours to depict its intensity or aspects, arrows to depict its direction, anything goes. Drawing or attempting to visually depict a problem or its solution can trigger off the brain into alternate neurological pathways to come up with better and more holistic ideas.

MENTAL GAME

Some of the simple games we played as children can help tone up the brain and reinforce the functions of sequential thinking, logic and the remembering of names and dates, crossword puzzle etc. offer an excellent mental workout as does a good round of scrabble.

MOVING BODY

Our bodies are very much a part of all our learning and learning is not an isolated brain function. Every nerve cell is a network contributing to our intelligence and our learning capability.

Complex movement stimulates complex thinking. Across the body arm movements such as those used in swimming or doing the march-past stimulate brain synchronization and help develop better communication across the hemisphere. Rhythmic movements such as dancing, skating, walking or martial arts also serve to stimulate the brain into activating more complex pathway.

IMPROVE FUNCTIONING OF RIGHT BRAIN HEMISPHERE BY FOLLOWING MENTAL/PHYSICAL EXERCISES

1 Visualise your organisation/home/yourself/spouse 10 years from now.

2 Redecorate your office/home, add toys, posters etc.

3 Design a logo for your job and family.

4 Make decisions based on intuition/gut feeling.

5 Conceptualize a new product.

6 Listen to music.

7 Take decisions as a team.

8 Convert words into pictures. Write a letter only through pictures (or with minimum words).

9 Learn to make a new dish.

10 Play with children the way they want to play.

11 Be with nature; enjoy watching the moon, the trees, the leaves, and the breeze.

12 Become spiritual (not necessarily religious).

13 Thank people, be grateful.

IMPROVING LEFT BRAIN HEMISPHERE BY FOLLOWING MENTAL/PHYSICAL EXERCISES

1. Learn a new computer program.

2. Define goals for the next year.

3. Prepare a time log.

4. Organise your filing system/desk.

5. Prepare a "to do "list and tick off things as you do them.

6. Plan a project and execute it in stages.

7. Be on time for appointments.

8. Use logic, probabilities, and data in decision making.

9. Write down all aspects of a practical retirement life.

10. Play logic games.

11. Assemble a model kit by following the instructions.

12. Organise books, files, audio tapes, and medicines at home category-wise.

13. Prepare a family tree.

14. Keep things neat and tidy in proper places.

15. Write down expiry dates of your driving license, insurance policy etc.

16. Write down advantages and disadvantages of a product decision and quantify them.

17. Complete tasks on time.

IV. ADOPT ALPHA STUDY METHOD

It is the key to store information for longer duration and also to recall it easily as and when required. Alpha state of mind is a level between sleep and wakefulness. While functioning at this level, apart from the usual left brain hemisphere activity, our right brain hemisphere also gets activated. This makes a person's thinking very powerful, very intuitive and very creative. This level connects us with our subconscious and helps us access the amazing powers lying dormant there. It has been found that any thought projected into the mind at this level will certainly be manifested in real life. This frequency is related to a relaxed state of mind, when one is free from the worries and frustrations of the physical world. They manifest when the rational mind and senses become inoperative and intuition is allowed to flow. Retention power is higher with alpha pattern of brain waves.

22

RECOLLECTION

Recollection is the most important function of memory. If there is no recollection, memory power will be termed very poor. Memory power means faster and accurate recall of stored information.

For quick and accurate recall you have to pay attention on followings:

I. PROPER REGISTRATION OF INFORMATION BY USING MEMORY TECHNIQUES

It is advised to register the information by creating memory triggers using memory techniques as explained in previous chapters. Strong impressions are created by mnemonic strategies of memory techniques only. Recollection becomes easier by memory triggers. Vague registration in memory makes it difficult to recollect the stored information.

II. REMAIN IN ALPHA STATE OF MIND

Alpha state of mind helps in quick and accurate recall of information as and when required. It not only helps in recalling but also helps to develop a positive personality. Following is its importance:

A. It makes our body healthy: Immunity level of the body goes up dramatically just by remaining in Alpha for 30 minutes daily. It releases stresses and helps in preventing heart disease. Miraculous healings have been experienced with this technique.

B. It enhances memory and concentration power: When you are at Alpha level of mind, your right part of brain is more active. It increases creativity and focusing ability.

C. It realizes our goal: It increases clarity of goals and helps in stepping towards achieving them. Things are always created twice, once in mind followed by the practical creation. If we can visualise the outcome powerfully, the manifestation becomes very easy.

D. It de-stresses us: There is a permanent cure of stress, depression, anger, frustration and disappointment; that one experiences. Alpha state of mind is nothing but pure bliss which creates stability of thoughts and wards off negative thoughts which produce negative emotions and negative attitude.

E. It solves insomnia problem: People, who had been using sleeping pills even for 20 yrs have stopped it after practising meditation and remaining at Alpha level. It helps to enjoy natural and rejuvenating sleep.

F. It helps to get rid of bad habits: At alpha we can talk to our own subconscious mind and create positive changes within us. Getting rid of bad habit by autosuggestion at Alpha level of mind is very easy and practicable by all.

G. It mends our relationship: At alpha level of mind, you can communicate with the sub conscious mind of others through telepathy and create positive changes there. This helps to mend relationships. Whatever you cannot speak to a person directly, can be communicated at Alpha level to his sub conscious mind. And the results are amazing.

H. It makes our personality charismatic: Remaining in alpha state of mind for longer duration instantly increases our charisma and draws the attention of others. It makes our personality positive and powerful. People around us start giving respect.

III HAVE A PROPER SLEEP (NOT MORE THAN SIX HOURS OF SLEEP)

Sleep is the most important factor for healthy living. Optimum hours of sleep one should have range between 5 to 7 hours. To manage our sleep, we must know same scientific facts.

SCIENTIFIC FACT ABOUT SLEEP

We sleep in cycles of 90 to 120 minutes each and our EEG indicates variety of waves during sleep ranging from alpha to delta. We spend first 50 % of each sleep cycle in light/ very light sleep, next 30 % in deep/ very deep sleep and rest 20% of the cycle in REM (Rapid Eye Movements) sleep (known as dream sleep).

We need to have a total of 45 to 50 minutes of delta waves to feel totally fresh after sleep. Our first two cycles carry about 20 minutes of delta waves in each cycle and the third cycle carries 5 to 10 minutes of delta waves only. After third cycle, delta waves are not produced at all.

Delta Waves are the deepest state of brain and primarily associate with holistic healing. The slowest brain wave, it is associated with deep sleep, Samadhi or cosmic consciousness. (To become consciously aware of this level one has to transcend the physical and mental planes, which lends itself to the ultimate goal of mankind-Realisation of the True Self). Recent scientific research is only now beginning to discover what yogis have known and practised for thousands of years- the fact that man has the ability to move his awareness consciously through the different levels of consciousness, thus opening up unlimited possibilities.

Sleeping after third cycle is either due to habit or for psychological satisfaction. But it is a waste of time because it never gives you relaxations, instead it drains out gained energy during three cycles and people feel tired even after sleeping more.

Sleep after third cycle is called half sleep or dream sleep, which produces more theta waves, which is a low amplitude wave with low frequency. Therefore one needs to have sleep only for three cycles. But two cycles sleep are also sufficient if needed. It refreshes you up for next 12 hours. After 12 hours you will feel to sleep one cycle, which again can freshen up for next 4 hours.

During deep sleep, we sleep completely in delta waves, where as in theta wave sleep (Dream sleep) our mind still works with imaginations but intellect does not function with its controlling power.

Therefore sleep means complete sleep with minimum 45 minutes of delta waves.

IV. REMAIN STRESS FREE (FREE FROM WASTE AND NEGATIVE THOUGHTS)

Stress, significantly reduces brain functions such as memory, intellectual efficiency and even brings premature old age. It affects our concentration and learning all of which are central to effective performance at work. Certain tests have shown up to 50 % loss of performance in cognitive tests performed by stress sufferers. Therefore it is advisable to remain stress free for better recollection.

V. PRACTISE RAJYOGA MEDITATION

The theta and delta state of mind is achieved by Rajyoga meditation in which mind remains fully awake but cut off from external world or sense organ perceptions and connected to either inner self or supreme source of infinite cosmic energy.

Half an hour of meditation can give the relaxation equal to one cycle of sleep and refreshes us for the next six hours. 15 to 20 minutes of meditation can refresh for next three to four hours.

Theta waves occur either in dream or at deep meditative level which bring about lasting changes. This is also known as the state of highest creativity when awake with these waves.

These waves are profusely emitted during sleep. They are associated with the unconscious mind and occur when deep unconscious data or impressions rise to the surface. Theta waves are manifested during deep states of meditation, intense creativity, ecstasy and receptivity to extra sensory perception. Control of the autonomic functions, such as heartbeat, digestion, bleeding etc. is possible while consciously functioning at this frequency. Thus recollection becomes easiest with the practice of Rajyoga Meditation.

[*You can learn the techniques of Rajyoga at any branches of Rajyoga Education and Research Foundation, a sisterly organisation of Brahma kumaris Ishwariya Vishva Vidyalaya (BKIVV), which have more than 6000 branches in our country.*]

23

IMPROVE YOUR MEMORY WITH DYNAMIC NEUROBICS

(Invisible doctor's dynamic neurobics helped me a lot on the journey to the Guinness World Records Biswroop Roy Chowdhary)-

Dr.Paul Nogier, a neurologist, spent around 20 years from 1950 to about 1970 in medical research and rediscovered that the ears correspond to the whole body. The ear corresponds to an inverted fetus curled in the womb. The ear lobe corresponds to the head. This fact was already known to the ancient Chinese acupuncturists and the great saints (rishis) in India.

The interest of Dr. Paul Nogier was stimulated when he came in contact of patients who claimed that they were relieved by having their ear punctured with a hot pin by a Middle Eastern woman. Dr.Nogier experimented and was surprised with the immediate relief of his patients.

Dr. Terry Oleson, Ph.D., from the University of California, Los Angeles and Dr.Jay Holder in Miami, Florida made further research and improvement on the work of Dr.Paul Nogier.

The great Indian rishis have developed a technique, to increase the intelligence of people based on the principle of ear acupuncture; unfortunately, the proper technique on, how to do this exercise has been distorted and lost.

To understand the principles, behind the dynamic neurobics, it is important to explain certain new scientific concepts. They are explained below.

• Bioplasmic body or energy body

Clairvoyants, with the use of their psychic faculties, have observed that the physical body is surrounded and interpenetrated by a luminous energy body. Just like the visible physical body, it has a head, two eye and two arms, etc. In other words, the energy body looks like the visible physical body. The energy body is called the bioplasmic body by Russian scientists.

The word bioplasmic comes from bio, which means life, and plasma, which is the fourth state of matter. The first three states of matter being solid, liquid, and gas. Plasma is ionized gas or gas particles with positive or negative charge. This is not the same as blood plasma. Bioplasmic body means a living energy body made up of invisible subtle matter.

To simplify the terminology we call bioplasmic body as "energy body". With the aid of Kirlian photography, scientists have been able to study, observe, and take pictures of small bioplasmic articles like bioplastic fingers, leave etc. It is through the energy body that prana or life energy is absorbed and distributed throughout the whole physical body.

• The function of the energy body

1. It absorbs, distributes, and energizes the whole physical body with prana (life energy), which nourishes the whole body so that it could, together with its different organs, function properly and normally. Without life energy, the body would die.

2. It acts as a mode or patron for the visible physical body. This allows the visible physical body to maintain its shape, form and features despite years of continuous metabolism. To be more exact, the visible physical body is modeled after the energy body. If the energy body is defective, then the visible body is defective. They are so closely related that what affects one, affects the other. If one gets sick, the other also gets sick. If one gets healed, the other also gets healed. This may manifest gradually or almost instantaneously, assuming there are no interfering factors.

3. The energy body, through energy centers or the chakras, controls and is responsible for the proper functioning of the whole physical body and its different parts and organs. This includes the endocrine glands, which are the physical manifestation of some of the major energy centers. A lot of sicknesses is caused partially by the malfunctioning of one or more energy centers.

4. The energy body, through its healthy rays and healthy aura, serves

as a protective shield against germs and diseased energy. Diseased energy, usedup energy, toxins, wastes are expelled by the health rays predominantly via the pores; thereby purifying the whole physical body.

• The meridians

Traditional Chinese medicine views subtle life energy (qi or chi) as taking the form of vibrational waves. The energy body has a front energy wiring and back energy wiring. In acupuncture this is called an energy channel or meridian. The front channel is called the conception channel, while the back channel is called the governor channel.

The life energy flows along the meridians. These channels form an intricate web through the body, like a second nervous system. It connects the physical body to the subtle energy bodies surrounding it.

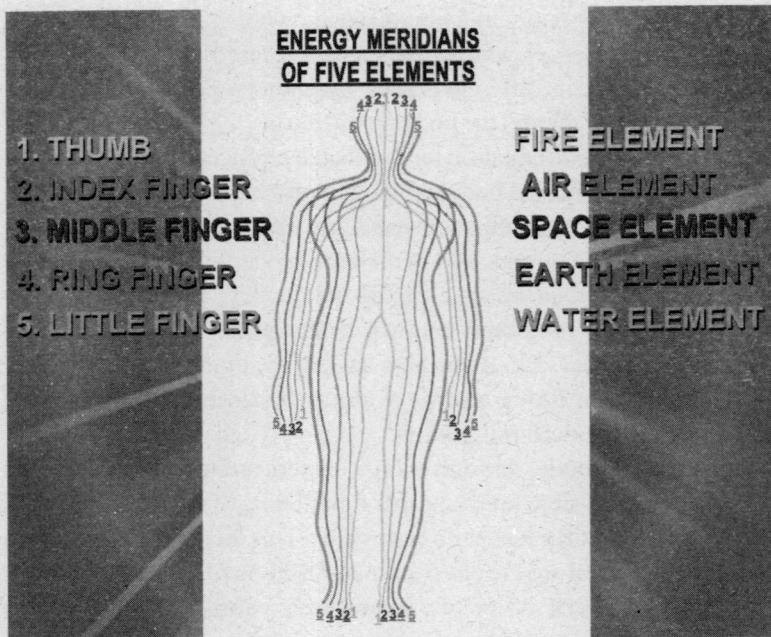

ENERGY MERIDIANS OF FIVE ELEMENTS

1. THUMB
2. INDEX FINGER
3. MIDDLE FINGER
4. RING FINGER
5. LITTLE FINGER

FIRE ELEMENT
AIR ELEMENT
SPACE ELEMENT
EARTH ELEMENT
WATER ELEMENT

•Expansion of energy body by connecting the tongue to the palate

Since the body has to eat, the front energy channel is broken in the mouth area. In order to make the energy wiring more complete, the tongue has to be connected to the palate. The tongue must be connected to the palate, to connect the front energy wiring, in order to complete the energy wiring in the front and back energy channels.

Energy channels have the capability of expanding and contracting. Based on clairvoyant observations, when the tongue is not connected to the palate, the front and back energy channels are about 2 millimeters in diameter.

When the tongue is connected to the palate, the front and back energy channels expand to about 5 to 10 millimeters in diameter.

• Energizing and activating both parts of the brain

The body has very complicated and subtle electronic equipment. The right ear lobe corresponds to the left brain while the left ear lobe corresponds to the right brain. To energize your brain do the followings: -

1. Activating left brain: - Gently squeeze the right ear lobe with the left thumb and left index finger with the thumb outside. When the right ear lobe is gently squeezed in this manner, it produces the necessary energy connection, which causes the left brain and pituitary gland to become energized and activated

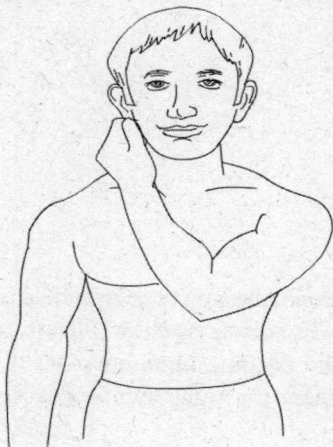

When seen clairvoyantly, the aura or energy field of the left brain and pituitary gland increases, by as much as 100% to 200%. he left brain and pituitary gland become luminous. But this condition is temporary; the moment the left thumb and the left index finger are removed from the right ear lobe, the left brain's and pituitary glands energy level goes back to its previous level. The left brain and pituitary gland become dim.

The results can easily be validated by pranic healers (Pranic Energy Healers) through scanning the left brain and the pituitary gland before squeezing the right ear lobe with left thumb and left index finger, during the squeezing, and after releasing the left thumb and left index finger from the right ear lobe.

2. Activating right brain: Gently squeeze the left ear lobe with the right thumb and right index finger with the thumb outside. When the left ear lobe is squeezed in this manner, it produces the necessary energy connection, which causes the right brain and pineal gland to become energized and activated.

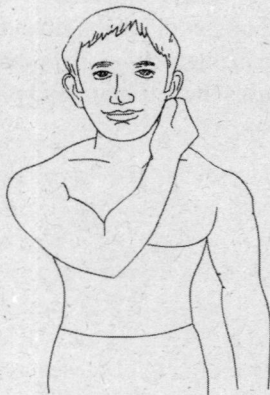

When clairvoyantly seen, the aura or energy field around the right brain and pineal gland increases by as much as 100% to 200%. The right brain and pineal gland also become luminous. But this condition is only temporary; the moment the right thumb and right index finger are removed from the left ear lobe, the energy level of the right brain and pineal gland goes back also to its previous level. They become dim.

These results can easily be validated by Pranic Healers (Pranic Energy Healers) through scanning the right brain and the pineal gland before squeezing the left ear lobe with right thumb and right index finger, during the squeezing and after releasing the right thumb and right index finger from the left ear lobe.

• Do not cause a short circuit by the wrong posture
If the left thumb and left index finger are used to gently squeeze the left ear lobe, it will cause a "short circuit". The right brain and pineal gland's energy level decreases and becomes depleted.

If the right thumb and right index finger are used to gently squeeze the right ear lobe, it will also cause a "short circuit." The left brain's and pituitary glands energy level decreases and becomes depleted. Using the wrong hand to gently squeeze the ear lobe has a depleting effect.

This means that if you use the right thumb and index finger to gently squeeze the right ear lobe, it will not work, because it is the wrong hand. If you use the left thumb and index finger to gently squeeze the left ear lobe, it will also not work, because it is the wrong hand.

• The correct posture
1 Correct finger position: - The thumb must be outside and the index finger must be inside when gently squeezing the ear lobe. This is the correct finger position. When the correct finger position is used, the pranic energy level of the brain is higher and the effect is more powerful than if the thumb is on the inside and the index finger is outside.

2 Correct arm position: - The right arm must be outside, while the left arm must be inside. This is the correct arm position. This will cause the brain to be energized and activated. It is seen clairvoyantly as the brain become more luminous.

The correct arm position applies to both male and female. If the right arm is inside and the left arm is outside, it causes a "short circuit" and the brain will become depleted and dimmer. This is the wrong arm position. Since the energy wiring connection is not correct, it will not have an energizing and activating effect on the whole brain.

If the wrong arm position is used, it will decrease the pranic energy level of the brain and the upper energy centers, while the pranic energy level of the lower energy centers will increase.

3. Correct directions: - It is as follows: -
(I) For children, teenagers and adults: - Children, teenagers and adults have a strong sex and basic energy centre. Therefore it is advisable to face the East for better results. East radiates predominantly violet pranic energy, which activates the upper energy centers. It facilitates the bringing up of energies from the basic energy center and sex energy center to the upper energy centers.
(II) For older people: - It is advisable to face the North when doing the dynamic neurobics, because their sex and basic energy centers are weak and depleted. Therefore, their lesser lower energies is to be transformed into higher energies, to be utilized by the upper energy centers and the brain. North radiates predominantly pranic energy.
Red prana energizes and strengthens, especially the lower energy centers. For younger people, it is not advisable to face the north because their lower energy centers are stronger.

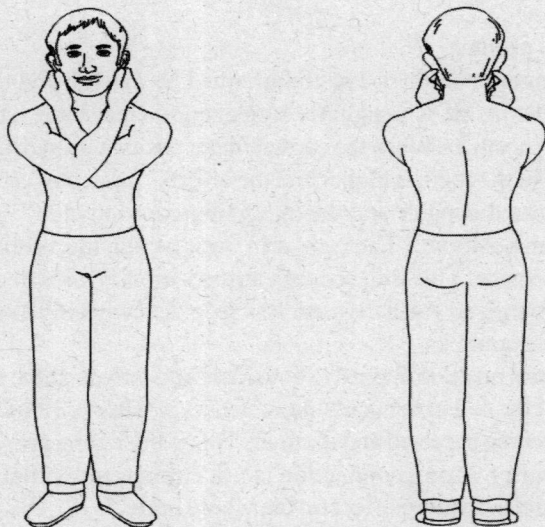

• Connect to divine source by visualizing deep blue (Indigo) colour

Dynamic neurobics gradually awaken the latent powers within us and also involve internal alchemy. Therefore, it is preferably safer and more effective to visualize first indigo colour and connect to the divine source for divine blessings. Divine rays of Indigo colour energise the brain and the complete nervous system.

• Dynamic neurobics is the best neuro muscular exercise for students
To transform the energies of the basic center and sex center into higher subtle energies to be utilized by the upper energy centers and the brain, it is necessary to squat in the correct posture. Do this exercise as follow: -

1. Stand in the correct posture facing the correct direction as per your age as explained above.
2. Connect to the divine source with colour visualization.
3. Sit down and inhale simultaneously, and when standing up exhale simultaneously.
4. Repeat 14 times per session.
5. For people, who need extra help to improve their intelligence, repeat 21 times per session.
6. For yogis, or people who do advanced meditation, repeat 7 times per

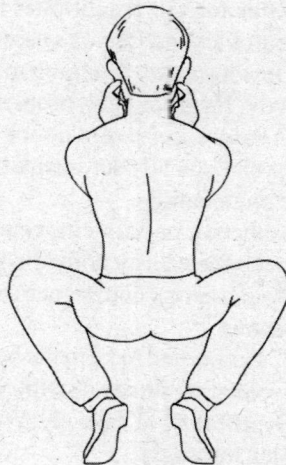

session only.

7   For people who are not so young or are physically handicapped, they can do dynamic neurobics in semisquat position, about 50-70 times per session. Doing the dynamic neurobics in semi-squatting is not as powerful as doing it in full squatting version. Therefore the number of times, should be increased in semi-squat position in order to get equivalent benefit.

8   Dynamic neurobics can be practiced, if necessary, twice or thrice a day. Over practice of this may cause congestion in the head area.

9   Release your fingers from your ear lobes.

This simple process of dynamic neurobics will bring the lower energies up to the upper energy centers. The lower energies are transformed into energies with much higher frequencies. These life energies of higher frequencies are utilized for energizing the brain, so it can function with greater efficiency and effectivity.

•Very Important Instructions while performing Dynamic Neurobics

1. Do not do dynamic neurobics two days before, during and two days after menstruation. During this period the sex energy center is filled with grayish energy. Doing this will bring the dirty energy to the upper energy centers and the brain.

2. If a person's sex energy center and basic energy centers are dirty, it is better for the practitioner to clean the centre by practicing light neurobics and Rajyoga before practicing the dynamic neurobics.

3. Do not smoke. Smoking makes dirty the physical body and energy body. It causes heart problems, hypertension and other problems.

4. Avoid excessive alcohol intake. Alcoholism is physically and psychologically detrimental to a person, and at the same time harmful to one's family.

5. Addictive or hallucinogenic drugs must be avoided because they make the energy body dirty and damage the physical body.

6. Avoid eating non vegetarian diets. They are very dirty for the energy centres.

7. It is important to keep the body clean and not overdo this exercise, to avoid or minimize possible physical health problems like: Insomnia, Overheating of the body, Weakening of the body, Pain & discomfort, Skin rashes etc.